REAL, RURAL

Real, Rural is Larry Meredith's memoir of "growing up rural" in Bushton, Kansas during the 1950s. It is a fascinating account of life in a small town (population 500-600) during the best of times for rural Kansas. Larry and many of his high school classmates fondly remember growing up in a community that provided all that was needed for a secure, happy life. They did not feel abandoned by a nation that was rapidly changing. Nor did they feel disadvantaged by the limitations of small-town life. However, they belonged to one of the last generations to enjoy the quiet, pastoral life of rural Kansas. Today, many of the once prosperous rural communities are invisible on the prairie landscape. Larry has done a masterful job of reminding us of what used to be.

> *Darrell Munsell, author of* From Redstone to Ludlow: John Cleveland Osgood's Struggle against the United Mine Workers of America, *retired university history professor and also a rural kid from Kansas*

If you grew up in the '50s, this book is a must read for you. If you weren't "Rural" you will wish you had been. The characters and times in this book are real; "Rural" was the place to have been in the '50s. Proud I was. It was a hoot!

> *Colonel Donnal Hiltbrunner (USMC Retired, Bushton, Kansas High School Class of 1956)*

Meredith nailed it with *Real, Rural*! For many of us in the '50s religious principles guided us in our actions. Reliance on others taught us teamwork and generosity. Striving for material goods meant working hard to earn them. Perhaps reviewing the past will help promote a new generation of hard-working, law-abiding individuals.

> *Myretta Behnke Bell (Bushton, Kansas High School Class of 1958)*

ALSO BY THE AUTHOR

THIS CURSED VALLY
This historical novel (1880-1930) is set in the valley
in which the author and his family now live,
and is based on a legend that the Ute Indians
placed a curse on the valley as they
were being driven to reservations
in the early 1880s.

**CAST A GIANT SHADOW: HOLLYWOOD
MOVIE GREAT TED WHITE
AND THE EVOLUTION OF
AMERICAN MOVIES AND TV
IN THE 20TH CENTURY**

REAL, RURAL
GROWING UP RURAL IN THE 1950S

LARRY K. MEREDITH

Raspberry Creek Books, Ltd.

Real, Rural
GROWING UP RURAL IN THE 1950S

Real, Rural is a work of nonfiction. Some names, dates and identifying details may have been changed or omitted.

© Copyright 2020 by Larry K. Meredith

All rights reserved.

ISBN: 978-0-9851352-8-7
Library of Congress Control Number: 2019957581

Printed in the United States of America

First Edition

info@raspberrycreekbooks.com

Raspberry Creek Books, Ltd.

Cover Design: by the author, photo of Groth family farmstead, central Kansas, around 1949 or '50 in the winter.

This book is in remembrance of
Miss Willa Holland, my high school English teacher,
and for all those adults who guided me through
my years of growing up rural. It is also for
my classmates who helped make those years
so special for me. Most importantly it is for
my parents, Lawrence and Eva Meredith, for my
sister, Linda Byers, and particularly for Ally,
my wife, who shared those growing up
years with me and joined me
in our journey into adulthood.
I especially want to recognize our daughter Suzy
Meredith-Orr and her husband Denny, our son Greg, his
wife Tina and our grandchildren Jack and Lauren
(Greg and Tina's children), all of whom
need to know and understand what
it was like when their parents and grandparents
were growing up in a world that was
far different from their own.

The 1950s and 1960s had been a period of enormous growth, the highest in American history, maybe in economic history.

Noam Chomsky

6 – REAL, RURAL

CONTENTS

Prologue – Before the Internet – p. 9
Chapter 1 – What Does "Rural" Mean? –p. 27
Chapter 2 – What is Kansas? –p. 45
Chapter 3 – Immigrants All – p. 53
Chapter 4 – An "Adequate" Education – p. 65
Chapter 5 – Camels in Kansas? – p. 77
Chapter 6 – Mickey, Marilyn and a Singer – p. 81
Chapter 7 – Stick Shifts, Studebakers & McCarthyism – p. 87
Chapter 8 – Everything We Need – p. 103
Chapter 9 – Not All Was Well in Rural Kansas – p. 113
Chapter 10 – A Rock in the Rear and 8mm Film – p. 119
Chapter 11 – That old Work Ethic – p. 135
Chapter 12 – Religion is Booming – p. 153
Chapter 13 – Jocks and Jockesses – p. 161
Chapter 14 – The Wind Comes Sweeping Down the Plain – p. 173
Chapter 15 – Time to "Light Out" – p. 177
Chapter 16 – And in Conclusion… – p. 183
Acknowledgements – p. 193
Reasons – p. 195
Bibliography – p. 197
About Us – p. 203

8 – REAL, RURAL

Prologue

Before the Internet

SKEETER CREEK WAS FLOODING. It gushed past the north side of the school building and over the Main Street in Bushton, Kansas, like the floods we heard about back East.

As it frequently did during the rainy season in the early 1950s, it had become a river of nasty and chocolaty brown water that we were sure was loaded with the occasional tree limb or two-by-four or various other dangerous items which our mothers feared would maim or kill one or more of us. The ugly flow blocked the town kids' route to school and made the morning commute of only a few blocks as exciting and adventurous as anything the Hardy Boys or Tom Sawyer ever encountered.

At least that's the way I remember it. Often after a heavy rain the aptly named Skeeter Creek rose out of its banks and water flowed across the street in front of the school in what was in reality probably only a shallow stream.

To some, it became a gigantic obstacle or at least a delay in the beginning of the school day. To others, it was simply a minor annoyance. Whatever it was, it was fun for a while.

In those days my classmates and I were "growing up rural." The small town of Bushton, Kansas, might have honestly claimed 500 or so people, a number of dogs and cats, a few other animals, large and small, and the occasional salesman or visitor from Kansas City or Chicago who came to try and sell something or to see a relative and to check out the deplorable conditions in which they were certain we lived. Add in nearby farm families and the population might well soar to maybe 600 or so – about as many as might occupy a square block or two in a city like Omaha or Toledo.

It didn't matter how badly off city folk thought I was. I

figured my life was just fine, thank you, and the thought of having to move to a city swarming with people I didn't know was not appealing to me. Oh, there were probably a few of my classmates who dreamed of city life and longed to be a part of the bustle that city dwellers appeared to enjoy, but not many. Most of us loved where we lived and appreciated the adults who taught us, coached us, protected us and ran the businesses that sold us the stuff we thought we needed.

No doubt, for some of us, "loved where we lived" is too strong a phrase. For those who didn't love the rural life, perhaps they accepted the life they lived and forged ahead because they had no choice. Nevertheless, we had access to the wide open plains of central Kansas, had good friends and generally didn't worry about too much.

Most of us knew we were rural and liked it that way. At least I did.

Even the occasional flooding of Skeeter Creek wasn't a big deal. Fortunately or unfortunately, depending on your point of view, whenever it happened, Acey Hall and another parent or two showed up in their pickups to ferry the stranded bikers and hoofers safely across the "raging torrent" for another day of education.

By the time football practice, or baseball or basketball or track and field, was over late in the afternoon, the flooded creek would have receded and my buddies and I could easily get to Delbert Henry's Bushton Drug on Main Street for a soft drink before making our way the remaining few blocks to our homes.

Neil Denton (Bushton High School class of '56) says his route home every evening after practice took him past the telephone office. The high school girl who was the part-time phone operator often called his parents to tell them "Neil is on his way home." There were few ways, if any, to be anonymous in a small town like Bushton.

Delbert Henry's Bushton Drug Store was a popular local store. It is now a museum. The soda fountain was great! The Post Office was to the right and it, too, is now part of the Museum.

Many of us were certain that city folk thought our circumstances were terrible and not nearly as good educationally as theirs because we were growing up in or near a small rural town. We weren't especially worried about it. Most of us, as far as I know, lived good lives, learned enough (and learned how to learn), didn't give much thought to the future but were being pretty well prepared for it, and somehow muddled into adulthood better off than we realized. Pretty much like city kids.

In the fall of 2019 a "philosophy" instructor at a west coast university took to Twitter to shame "rural Americans" and those who aren't "pro-city."

"I unironically embrace the bashing of rural Americans," wrote the instructor (actually a graduate student but I won't give him more publicity by using his name or his university). He said "they, as a group, are bad people who have made bad life decisions…and we should shame people who aren't pro-city." He also suggested that rural citizens should have higher healthcare costs, pay more in taxes and be forced to live an "uncomfortable" life for rejecting "efficient" city life.

That's pretty much what those of us who love the rural life expect to hear from city folk who have never had the pleasure of driving a tractor and working some of the most fertile farmland in the U.S., never drove a pickup down a gravel road with a pretty girl as a passenger and a big dog sitting between the two of you like he thought he belonged there, never enjoyed the tranquility and downright pleasure of fishing a small stream all by yourself, and never had the comfort of knowing all your neighbors and trusting them to be there for you when help was needed.

As to "efficient" city life, that can be debated. Rural people can easily haul out statistics to suggest that quite a few cities are somewhat less than efficient in the use of tax dollars and in providing for all citizens.

Many online responses to the grad student's comments were not kind and frequently rather profane.

Fortunately, almost immediately after the grad student's comments went viral, many pundits in the print press and on radio and television rose to the defense of rural America. "We started as a rural country," one said. "We remain at our heart linked to rural communities. Thank goodness for small towns, farms and traditional values."

Despite all those efforts by that poor grad student and other misguided city folks, I'm sure many city people still dream of finding the perfect place in the country where they can live quiet lives, raise their children in safety and become something like the gentlemen farmers of historic fiction who are rich and wise and know just the right thing to do or say at all times.

Not so fast! It's not that easy. Living in rural America has both positive and negative aspects. And it's lots of hard work. What I recall are mainly the positive aspects. I am who I am thanks to the environment in which I grew up. Want'a argue? I'm game.

* * * *

In his 1987 book of essays entitled *Owning it All* (published by Graywolf Press) author William Kittredge suggested that during his childhood he and most of his classmates believed the actual world was made up only of the high desert country of southeastern Oregon. The rest of creation, he opined, was as distant as news on the radio.

Forget for a moment that Kittredge is writing about the state of Oregon. Substitute, instead, something like "we clearly understood the skillet-flat farmland of central Kansas as the actual world" and I believe you will describe the way many, perhaps most, of my classmates, felt about where they lived. At least you would be describing my personal understanding. Bushton and Rice County, Kansas, did make up "the actual world" to me and, frankly, that was enough.

My classmate Mildred (Peterson) Dundas (class of '57) spoke for many of us when she said "living in a small town was all I knew as I lived in Bushton until I went to college." Whether we went away to college or to a job or a marriage, Rice County Kansas was, indeed, all most of us knew.

The rest of creation, as Kittredge termed it, was brought to us through books, movies and the radios we listened to in our homes and in our vehicles.

Some of the farm kids had pickup trucks but pretty much whatever we drove in those days had a radio. In my family's cars the radio was often tuned to KVGB in Great Bend but if that station was featuring music that was less "cool" than I wanted I could easily find another station that was playing Buddy Holly or Jerry Lee Lewis or the Everly Brothers or Fats Domino. Sometimes when my folks were driving and I didn't have control of the radio or when my sister Linda (Meredith) Byers (class of '60) wanted something less raucous, we were forced to listen to the latest news or even Teresa Brewer.

Somehow we were exposed to a world that appeared to be vastly different from the one in which we lived. After being exposed to that world, most of us were still happy that we lived where and how we did.

As I write this I've just returned from a weekend trip to Denver, normally a three-hour drive from our home. Thanks to a heavy snowfall and accidents on Interstate 70 it took us seven hours to make the drive. We went to see an exhibit of Monet paintings and to hear a Mannheim Steamroller concert. Those events were worth the trip. We're glad to have those opportunities and others such as Colorado Rockies baseball games, other exhibits, plays, musical events and shopping, but it is always a relief for me to return to the quietness of home, the lack of heavy traffic and to a level of stress that is reasonable and more easily managed than I find in most cities.

From here on when a year is set off (such as '57) in a

parenthetical phrase it indicates the year the person being referenced graduated from Bushton High School. A woman's maiden name follows her first name, also in parentheses.

Joy (Long) Nickerson ('55) said her family's entertainment centered a great deal around the radio. "Many evenings after supper we would all sit around the radio and listen to programs such as *Fibber McGee and Molly* and *The Lone Ranger*," she said.

I remember sitting in our kitchen near the radio while my mother ironed or did other chores that mothers did in those days, listening to whatever program she had turned on. Often, it was programs such as *The Shadow* or (like Joy's family) *Fibber McGee and Molly* or even *The Bell Telephone Hour*.

I also recall being forced to listen to the 1952 Democratic Party Convention coverage which seemed to go on for weeks although it was only from July 21-26. In case you've forgotten, Estes Kefauver had the most delegates after the first round of voting but President Truman came out in support of Adlai Stevenson and Stevenson was nominated on the third ballot. It was the last nomination contest of either major political party in the U.S. to require more than one round of voting to nominate a presidential candidate to date. On Tuesday, November 4, 1952, however, Republican Dwight D. Eisenhower (a Kansan) won a landslide victory over Stevenson and ended a string of twenty years of Democratic Party wins.

I'm not sure but, overhearing whispered conversations between my parents when they thought I might be close enough to hear them, I think they cancelled each other's vote that year with one voting for Stevenson and the other for Ike. But I could be wrong.

During the fifties I was mainly concerned with school, church, sports and a pretty blue-eyed dark-haired girl who was a year younger than me. I'm sure my classmates and I had no idea that the most significant decade of our growing-up years was to go down in history as essentially boring and plain but was, in actuality, so very important to the following years and decades.

Author David Halberstam, in his 1993 book *The Fifties* (published by Open Road Integrated Media) suggests that because activities of the fifties were reported to us in black and white, usually by still photographers, the pace of the decade seemed slow, almost languid compared to the decade that followed, the '60s, which was more often than not caught in living color on tape or film.

Nevertheless, the era was a much more interesting one than it appeared on the surface. Exciting new technologies were being developed and many people were already beginning to question the purpose of their lives and Halberstam wondered whether that purpose had become too much about material things.

Personally, I didn't worry too much about material things. I really didn't need much and I knew that my family couldn't afford a great deal in the way of frills and doodads that would have been nice to have but that we didn't need or have room for. Just like a lot of city folk, I'm sure.

We were rural but I didn't know any "bad people" like those described by that grad student at a west coast university. We lived life fully, did what needed to be done and grew into full-fledged adults, many of whom made significant contributions to the society in which we live.

Some historians say the *political* decade of the fifties began with either the end of World War II in 1945 or the start of the Korean War in 1950 and ended with the escalation of the Vietnam War in the early 60s. Others say it includes the period between V-J Day to the Kennedy Assassination (1945 to 1963). Still others point out that, *culturally* speaking, it started with the beginning of *I Love Lucy* in 1951 and ended with the release of *Psycho* in 1960.

Exciting changes in this period include the exhilarating time when tailfins on cars got REALLY wild, when women's skirts got shorter, when Rock & Roll was being heard more and more on radio and when the first of the Baby Boomers reached Junior High.

No big auto tailfins but I like this photo of my Dad and me.

Automobile tailfins were, indeed, getting much wilder but that didn't necessarily mean the cars were getting any better. In fact, while GM was the Colossus of auto manufacturers, and probably of most producers of other products, they were concentrating more on style and less on engineering. But we loved the classy look of the cars of the fifties and no doubt simply assumed they ran better because they were newer.

In the meantime throughout the decade we were hearing ominous comments that made all of us nervous, perhaps especially the parents of young men whom their parents feared would soon be required to join a branch of the military and fight and perhaps die in the world's most disastrous war.

In 1956 Dwight D. Eisenhower said: "We are in the era of the thermonuclear bomb that can obliterate cities and can be delivered across continents. With such weapons, war has become, not just tragic, but preposterous."

Despite that kind of rhetoric, for many of us much of the decade meant looking forward to becoming **high school seniors** and, therefore, adults, or nearly so at least, and considering college or a job and/or possible marriage and parenthood.

Donnal Hiltbrunner ('56) said "turning 18 was a biggie in Bushton. You could now go to work for Northern Natural Gas." Working at "Northern" was a kind of rite of passage for the boys of Bushton. Don said most of the town guys worked summers there during college, and others would graduate and spend a career there.

Never mind that Gen. Lewis B. Hershey, Selective Service Director 1942-1970, famously said: "a boy becomes an adult three years before his parents think he does, and about two years after he thinks he does."

Most of us were aware of the fact that important events were happening politically, scientifically, athletically, spiritually, militarily, culturally and even educationally but few of us who were growing up then and even some adults, including many of the country's leaders, had an inkling of the actual world-changing significance that many of those events foretold.

For example, the U.S. came out of World War II with little or no rebuilding to do and was one of the few nations in that condition. The focus was on innovation, so science and industry were at the forefront of potential change. Also, it's no coincidence that Disneyland, the embodiment of optimism, opened in 1955, and "Tomorrowland" promised a "great big beautiful tomorrow."

In October of 1957 the launch of Sputnik started the Space Race and made many of us downright nervous. This was the point where science fiction dreams suddenly became a part of government policy.

There were other things going on in the fifties that we youngsters should have been aware of and perhaps many more of my classmates than I realize were, indeed, paying attention to. Personally, I'm sure I had other things on my mind. Here are some of the things for which the fifties are, or should be, remembered:

1950: credit cards were invented. The first was Diner's Club cards, made of cardboard; the Korean War began

1951 and 1952: inventions included diet soda, super glue and roll-on deodorant; polio vaccine was created

1953: DNA was discovered; color TV made its debut

1954: the first atomic submarine; the Brown v. Board of Education nation-changing decision in Topeka, Ks. and the beginning of the Civil Rights movement; birth control pills trials began; cigarettes were reported to cause cancer; microwave oven invented; automatic doors made their first appearance

1955: Velcro invented; James Dean died in an automobile accident

1956: Ultrasound and TV remotes were invented

1957: Birth control pills became widely available

1958: The microchip was invented; the North American Air Defense Command (NORAD) established a radar system close to the North Pole in an effort to detect and, hopefully, forestall Soviet attacks on the U.S.

1959: Three-point seatbelts were invented

There was a great deal more than that, of course, such as the fact that two-thirds of all new cars purchased in the fifties were bought on credit, South Vietnam was attacked by Viet Cong Guerrillas and troops were sent to Arkansas to enforce anti-segregation laws.

One writer called the '50s "a decade of idealistic fever that burned after World War II." From all the activity during that decade, that thought appears to have hit the mark.

* * * * *

Meanwhile, back in Bushton, Kansas –

The Bushton Rural High School class of 1957 had only twelve graduating students. I was one of them.

The Bushton High Trojans

Class of '57. In case you can't read the names they are top from left: Jay Huebner, Mildred (Peterson)Dundas, Betty (Schroeder) Dohrman, Marian (Voss) McKay, Larry Meredith; Second Row Ray Huebner, Sponsor and Coach Calvin Winter, Superintendent Paul Ridgway, Eugene Hoelscher; Third Row, Phil Henry, Shirley Mullenix, Gary Prosser, Connie (Rhoades) Stern and John Heinz.

Attending a 60th reunion were, standing, Mildred (Peterson) Dundas, Kansas (hostess); Jay Huebner, Florida; Jo (Lindsay) Hodges (California); Connie (Rhoades) Stern (Minnesota). Seated, Larry Meredith (Colorado) and Ray Huebner (deceased) (Texas). Also attending but not pictured was Marian (Voss) McKay (Kansas).

Nobody in Bushton or the nearby farmers who sent their kids to the school thought the small senior class was unusual or even especially interesting. The school was important but so was the weather and getting the custom cutters lined up for wheat harvest in June and the free movies shown outdoors on humid bug-infested summer nights and driving to the two-block-long unpaved main street late on Saturday afternoons and sitting in or on your car and saying "hello" or "howdy" or "good to see you" to your friends and neighbors with whom you hadn't visited for a day or so.

There wasn't much in the way of television in those days – what we had was from stations in Wichita and not many of us had TV sets in our homes until well into the decade – so weekend evenings were spent with friends and relatives, schoolmates, girlfriends or boyfriends, ballgames, school activities, games in the vacant lot next door, maybe going to the drive-in at Lyons. Some of us even read books. Others sat in or on their cars downtown and watched to see who else didn't have anything else to do.

Many of the farm kids, though, worked their fields on tractors until late, threw rectangular hay bales weighing 50 to 75 pounds from the ground to flatbed trailers, did other chores and generally worked as field hands or housekeepers for their farmer parents. Many in town either felt sorry for them or admired the ways they dealt with grownup responsibilities.

Some people were even concerned with politics, but not much.

Nobody worried too much about the competition between the two grocery stores on Main Street and they drove to Lyons or Great Bend (about 20 and 30 miles away) to do their "serious" shopping. Bill Volkland's Bushton State Bank took care of whatever money anyone had. Almost every small town had a doctor in those days and the health center and the dentist dealt with the sore backs and toothaches people brought to them. The library was open often and long enough to meet our literary needs and Nickerson's farm implement supply made sure the proper tractors and combines were available and in good working order at the right time. The grain elevator was the tallest structure in the town and also the busiest during harvest. The Huebners even had a pool hall that was mysterious and intriguing to the young boys of the town while most of the girls pretended it wasn't there. Cecil Dalzel kept the sidewalk swept in front of his barber shop and the service station sold a gallon of gasoline for less than 30 cents.

The twelve members of the class of '57 never gave their small number a second thought. In fact, when Wayne Groth graduated in 1961 his class also had only 12 members. Wayne said "when some of my friends now talk of their high school days and the matter of size of their high school class comes up, I can usually be the winner by having the smallest." He said his granddaughter recently stated she had about 500 in her senior class and he was happy to tell her of his class size and the fact that he knew everyone by name. "Of course," he said, "she couldn't do the same for her class."

In Bushton's high school everyone was a friend and, though the actual words weren't used and no one might have even thought of using them, I believe we loved and trusted one another like family. Even the Catholics and Protestants got along just fine as far as I knew.

Actually, the small class was, in many ways, a Godsend. Everybody did everything. We played sports, participated in school plays, took our turns at being class officers and some played in the band. All the boys were "jocks" and even some of the girls. In those days no one would have been considered a "nerd" or a "scholar" (whatever the word might have been back then) even though some in the class made better grades than the others.

It simply didn't matter.

The junior class in 1957 had 31 students but only five boys. That was just fine with me because that pretty blue-eyed girl was one of the 31 and I was an "older man" and not one of the "boys" in her class.

The entire high school totaled fewer than 90 students and still the hallways seemed downright crowded between classes.

During those carefree days everything revolved around the school or the churches. A Methodist church in town and another Methodist Church in the country brought out the Protestants on Sunday mornings while a Catholic Church sat stately in the countryside and attracted members on Saturday nights or Sunday mornings. Other denominations were represented with churches in nearby towns.

I was a Methodist because there was no Baptist Church in town and also because that pretty blue-eyed girl attended the Methodist Church regularly with her parents. Her mother played the organ and her father was a member of the choir and the official board. We loved official board meetings after Sunday evening services because we sat together barely a block away on her grandmother's porch and "visited" while her father was in a meeting.

In those days, the 1950s, Bushton was, for the most part, a well-kept town with nicely maintained homes, mowed lawns, smooth streets and obvious pride of ownership whether of a home or a business. Often when I visited a similar small town, perhaps to visit a distant relative or to play a ballgame against the town's high school, I was disappointed to find that community didn't measure up to Bushton's standards of neatness.

Maybe I just saw the wrong part of that town. Or maybe not.

Many of the students at that time lived on farms and either drove their own cars to school or were "bussed" in by an area farmer or farmer's wife who drove a vehicle holding maybe eight passengers.

The pretty young girl with intense blue eyes was one of those passengers.

My sister Linda, our parents and I lived in the northern part of town. Linda and I rode our bicycles or walked the few blocks to school on the southern edge. Most of us even liked school.

Looking back, I owe a great deal to all of my teachers (more on some of them later) but perhaps especially to a small woman we affectionately referred to as "Banty." Miss Holland was our English teacher and somehow got me interested in the written word. In fact, she once saw to it that I got a byline in the school's mimeographed newspaper for an article I wrote (only a few paragraphs) in which I urged everyone to "play fair." It was a thrill and it might have had something to do with the fact that I would eventually major in journalism at Kansas State College (now Kansas State University – K-State) in Manhattan.

Miss Willa Holland ("Banty") -- photo scanned from the yearbook

Now, more than 60 years later, that pretty blue-eyed girl from the class a year behind me (her name then was Alyce Lyn Groth) is just as beautiful as she was then. I called her Ally. Still do after all these years of marriage. Our relatives, friends and fellow church members have adopted the name "Ally" as well. Several of my classmates (like that pretty blue-eyed girl who is now my wife) have hung on to their youthful beauty. Some have died. Most of those women have married, changed their names and now have children and grandchildren. Some even have great grandchildren.

Even in the '50s rural America was changing. Though many of us didn't realize it, those changes were being forced upon us.

My author friend Darrell Munsell, who also grew up in rural Kansas, reminded me that technology was spurring efficiency and reducing the number of people needed for agriculture.

That, Darrell said, changed the whole economy of small town America, forcing young people to head to the cities for job opportunities. This, Darrell believes, is the real story of today's small town America.

Ally and me at a K-State fraternity dance in 1956

I took this portrait of my sister Linda as part of a photography class at K-State.

Most of my classmates from those days have moved to towns nearby or are scattered across the country in exotic locations such as Texas or Florida. Now and then many of those who are able-bodied get together at "all-school reunions" or for special events such as 60-year anniversaries (or shorter or longer), and often need photo nametags to help with identification.

How did we young people survive growing up so rural? How did so many of us manage to live productive and significant lives with a Bushton background and such a limited and bare (city people thought) education? And how do the memories flow so easily?

Today, with the ubiquitous World Wide Web we have access to information that covers practically anything we want to know, and much we'd rather not know, and it's relatively easy to find plenty of information about life in the fifties and, thus, start those memories flowing as never before.

For example, the "Fabulous Fifties," as portrayed on TV and in movies, according to the website https://tvtropes.org, are described in the typical view of the era as one of pink pressboard suburban houses filled with apron-clad housewives. All the men wear slippers and smoke pipes. All the girls are teenaged and wear poodle skirts, and all the boys are freckle-faced scamps with slingshots in their pockets. Parents evidently all sleep in separate beds and kiss each other only on the cheek.

In media, there are three versions of The Fifties. The first is how the time was portrayed in works that were actually made then. In this version, the fifties were a suburban paradise where everyone was always happy, either forgetting the bad events that happened during the last decade or reminiscing about the prosperous times of previous years. And there were no problems except for all those juvenile delinquents running around or if the nearest college had some commies spreading un-American values or stories that flying saucers were landing.

The next version was the "nostalgic fifties" as portrayed in the '70s and '80s. By then the teenagers of the fifties suddenly became the heroes. This led us to believe that all the teenagers back then hung out at the local malt shop where a jukebox played nothing but hits. The girls were only "seemingly" wholesome and both sexes were experiencing their own coming of age stories and could be found necking in cars at the drive-in theatre.

Finally, there are the "historical fifties." The nostalgic fifties by then were dying out because fewer and fewer writers in Hollywood actually remembered the fifties. Those who were the children of those former teens took a very jaundiced view of the era. Because of that, today's films and TV shows about the fifties tend to deal more with the political issues of the era – civil rights and McCarthyism, for example – and less with teen culture. Thus the decade is now filtered more through a political or ideological lens than a nostalgic one and teenagers aren't the only people who matter.

Robert P. Jones, in *The End of White Christian America*, says of America, after the hardships and victories of World War II and before the cultural upheavals of the 1960s, that June

Cleaver was its mother, Andy Griffith was its sheriff, Norman Rockwell was its artist and Billy Graham and Norman Vincent Peale were its ministers.

However it was measured, the decade of the fifties was a critical one for me. My Dad was home from the war that had ended in the previous decade, I was growing into the person I would become as a young adult and later as an older one, I was discovering what interested me other than Ally, and the world around all of us, rural though it was, was shaping up to offer opportunities and challenges that would define who all of us would become.

I loved Bushton. I loved the ruralness of central Kansas. I felt that I was where I belonged and I was beginning to have a glimmer of what I would become and how I would fit into the world that awaited me.

Not everyone felt that way. I know that some of my classmates felt the life they had was unfair, boring and, to some, frightening. A few were right and they would never be able to deal effectively with the world in which they would ultimately exist as an adult. I understand that, and I am saddened because of it. However, I was fine with the way life was treating me and in my world at that time I was content. In fact, a Sunday school teacher told me a story about a Biblical character who said he had learned to be content in whatever situation he found himself. I tried to emulate that.

In the 1950s, my classmates and I were, indeed, growing up rural. At the same time, we were part of a large extended family of young relatives, friends and acquaintances throughout the country who were struggling through the same throes of adolescence, rural or urban, wondering if we were missing something by living where we did and, like every other youngster in the world, facing disappointment, dealing with success, discovering how to be a part of a group, learning about envy and greed, accepting who and what we were and figuring out how to change, or if change was even necessary.

Chapter 1

What Does "Rural" Mean?

Down a country road...

GROWING UP IN BUSHTON I don't recall thinking that I needed to change or that my life needed changing in any way. We knew about large cities, of course, and at least some of us felt sorry for the people who had to live in them. Many of us considered that the noise must be awful and the intense traffic would mean we couldn't ride our bikes with such abandon. At the time, I thought of city life as teeming like a colony of busy beetles when a large flat rock was turned over out in a pasture or like an upset bunch of ants when their anthill is disturbed. And the crime! I don't recall that Bushton had any crime at all. We had a city policeman but I doubt that he was very busy. My Dad was elected to the City Council a time or two and I remember he was called out one evening to help send a door-to-door salesman on his way when it was determined that the man was breaking a city statute forbidding his kind of sales (whatever they were). We also had a School Board, of course, and Ally's father Vernon served on it. I'm sure there were other boards and commissions but I assumed they had little or no impact on me.

So why consider changing?

Later years would indicate that most of us were prepared well-enough for a future that would bring massive change, more wars, political angst and the requirement for major decision-making that would dramatically affect our lives.

When we were growing up in rural America we didn't have any problem knowing what "rural" meant. Since then the government has made a science of studying the "ruralness" of the country and, no doubt, has poured a great deal of tax-payer money into the effort. All that money and research has come up with some astounding information.

Believe it or not, the U.S. Census Bureau, possibly after years of debate, defines "rural" as *"what is not urban – that is, after defining individual urban areas, rural is what is left."* Somebody made a great deal of money with that definition.

On a website titled theconversation.com, dated February of 2017 we find a startling statement that suggests rural people and issues generally receive little attention from the urban-centric media and policy elites. Few of us need reminding of that very obvious fact. However, the website later redeems itself by crediting rural America with many unique contributions to the nation's character and culture as well as providing most of its food, raw materials, drinking water and clean air. The site claims rural America is a deceptively simple term for a remarkably diverse collection of places. It says [*In 2017]* it included nearly 72 percent of the land area of the U.S. and 46 million people.

Farms and farmers make up a large percentage of the country's rural area and population. I suspect that a large majority of the rest of the American population has no idea of the "business" side of farming. A farm is, and has always been, a *business* requiring a significant investment, not only to get started but also to stay in operation through the lean years as well as the profitable ones. From the website http://nationalfestivalofbreads.com we learn such facts as:

On average, Kansas is the largest wheat producing state. Nearly one-fifth of all wheat grown in the United States is grown in Kansas. No longer are Kansas and other states in the Great Plains considered to be situated in the "Great American Desert." Now we're the "Breadbasket of the World."

Kansas has about 60,000 farmers, including almost 7,900 women farmers, and annual average wheat production in Kansas for the past five years has been about 328 million bushels.

The barn on the Groth farm.

Sketch of the farmhouse.

Ally's grandparents Harry and Dola Groth with her aunt Loma.

Sue Habiger, Ally and her brother Wayne.

Bushton quilters, from left: Lydia Beeman, Lucy Murphy, Esther Durr, Lela Holland, Elsie Boldt, Edna Dressel, Anne Blank, not identified, Dola Groth, Pearl Huckstep and Jenny Hemmer

Vernon Groth on the hay wagon with his helper Sport the family dog.

The website estimates that all the wheat grown in Kansas in a single year would fit in a train stretching from western Kansas to the Atlantic Ocean.

Kansas is number one in flour milling in the U.S. One bushel of wheat provides about 42 pounds of white flour, enough for about 70 one-pound loaves of white bread. Each American consumes about 134 pounds of wheat flour every year.

Buying a combine these days is somewhat akin to buying a house. Although there wasn't the demand for equipment as large as today's in the '40s and '50s, according to the website https://livinghistoryfarm.org [*today*] a tractor will *start* maybe at $150,000, a combine at $240,000. With all the demands on farmers to continue to produce more efficiently and not rely upon government plans and/or government subsidies, it's amazing that they can continue to exist.

A farmer's wife named Dorothy, the site reports, was perfectly capable of getting on a tractor and disking a field if need be. Many farmers' wives around Bushton did, and still do, just that. She also took a variety of part-time jobs to help make ends meet on the farm or to buy additional equipment. She believed that on a farm, the woman was the helping hand and a partner. But she indicated she would rather be the woman than the man. She said she couldn't take some of the pressure that the man takes. She worries about it, but always figures he'll take care of it like he always does.

Ally's father Vernon Groth maneuvers his combine during a wheat harvest.

The website believes there is no better life than a farmer's life. But it wonders whether or not he or she can remain on the farm. Thirty years ago, there were about 7 million farms. Today fewer than 3.5 million farms feed 53 percent more people.

Way back in 1790 more than 90 percent of the U.S. population was "rural." By 1920, that number had dwindled to only 50 percent and, according to the Census Bureau, today only about 15 percent of the population resides in rural counties.

Most rural counties are still experiencing persistent population decline and the small town of Bushton, which is becoming smaller, and which is part of Rice County, Kansas, is illustrative of that fact.

Bushton never got very large. It might have reached its peak in 1950 when the census recorded a population of 532 hardy souls. Add in the nearby farming families and there might have been 600 or 700 (more or less) people who claimed Bushton as their town. By 1960 the census recorded 499 Bushton residents and in 2010 it was down to 279.

Millions of people have left rural areas over the past century because of, among other things, growing opportunities in urban areas. The message has been clear: more people have left rural areas than have arrived and fewer young women have remained to bear children. As a result, deaths have exceeded births, further spurring a downward spiral of population decline.

Statistics show there were brief periods when the rural population rebounded, mainly in the 1970s and the 1990s. However, as the Census Bureau indicates, between 2000 and

2015, the rural population grew by just 3.1 percent. Urban areas grew by 16.3 percent.

Nevertheless, I am proud of the fact that I grew up "rural" and that I was a member of that part of the country.

In 1948, when I was in the fourth grade and the war in Europe had ended only a few years earlier, my family moved to Bushton. Dad, recently discharged from the Army, had been transferred from a Jones and Laughlin Supply store (oil field equipment) in Russell, Kansas, to the store in Bushton and became a field salesman, a promotion from a store manager. We had moved from Oklahoma to Kansas when I was in the first grade and lived in the tiny town of Gorham, a few miles west of Russell, until my folks found a place in Russell itself. My family and I have driven by Gorham on Interstate 70 many times in recent years and it is smaller (WAY SMALLER) than Bushton. That hardly seems possible but it's true. Russell itself, in the 40's, had a population of around 5,000, two movie theatres with wonderful Saturday afternoon matinees of what seemed like every possible Western movie ever made, some industry and a Main Street with clothing stores, pharmacies and just about everything else one would want or need. Today, Russell County is still one of the leading petroleum producing counties in Kansas.

As I recall, moving to Bushton was not traumatic for me. In fact, I was overjoyed when I was welcomed to the town the day we were moving into our house near the grain elevator on the north side of town.

Those who so quickly welcomed me to town were several neighbor boys who might have been about my age and included Ted Hall and Robert Packer and others. They came over as a group while we moved our furniture into the house, and invited me to "come and play" with them. Both Ted and Robert would ultimately move away and I have sadly lost touch with both of them.

I recall being relieved and happy that it appeared it would be easy to make friends in Bushton – and it truly was. A big vacant lot just south of my house (which came with the house) helped as we used it for youthful neighborhood gatherings for football, basketball and baseball games, depending on the season, and for everything else when a bunch of us got together. My Dad put up a basketball goal out there on an area of hard-packed dirt and even when there were no other kids around I could find a basketball or a volleyball that had enough air in it, and shoot baskets.

Some of the neighborhood gang including, from left, Ron Huebner and his little brother Dennis, Larry Meredith (the tall guy), in front of him Billy Long and, standing to the right is Donald Long, known as "Ducky." Ron grew taller than Larry.

There were some who considered we lived on the wrong side of the tracks but the thought never bothered me. My sister Linda (Meredith) Byers ('60) said "I guess you could say that we lived at the corner of Peek and Plumb, or *Peek around the corner and you're Plumb out of town!*"

In my memory, the house we lived in was much larger than it actually was. We lived there only a few years but I recall wonderful details that I'm sure will linger in my mind forever. The front door, as in many homes in those days, and maybe even today, was seldom used. The house faced west but we entered via the side door – the one on the south. That was because the detached single-car garage was out that door, as was the small chicken house. When friends or relatives came to call they may have been directed to the front door but I kind of doubt it.

The "old" house looking east at the front door.

The "old" house with the Studebaker in the driveway.

The south door had a very bright yard light mounted just above it. One summer night in maybe '55 or '56 my close friend Neil Denton dropped me off after a baseball game in a neighboring town. It was stifling hot and the two of us had stripped down out of those heavy and hot baseball uniforms to nothing but our jockey straps. As I was halfway between Neil's car and the house my mother flipped on the yard light and I was fully exposed to the world – nearly naked! She thought it was downright funny.

As I think back, we lived on the edge of town and on the south side of the house there were no neighbors, only the railroad. So it was doubtful that anyone saw me "in the flesh" so to speak.

Anyway, just inside that south door was the kitchen/dining room. It might have been the largest room in the house and it was used for almost everything. I have some photos of the smaller living room which welcomed anyone who came in the front door but I can't find any of the kitchen/dining room.

The one bathroom we had (with a tub and no shower) was off the kitchen on the north side. Some of my classmates say they didn't yet have indoor plumbing but I don't recall any time when we didn't have a "regular" indoor bathroom.

My parents' master bedroom was also just off the kitchen. It was on the southwest and separated from the living room by a thin wall and a stairway to the second floor. Because my parents wanted both my sister Linda and me to take piano lessons, they bought an old upright piano but the only place it would fit was in their own bedroom. That's where we practiced. We took piano lessons from Ruth Clair for a few years and I finally quit when the lessons began to interfere with football practice. Mrs. Clair's studio was in her farmhouse a couple of miles west of town. I learned just enough music to "be dangerous," as they say, but Linda continued and has become a good pianist and, I'm sure, organist. The fact that I could read music was a help in the church choir or when trying to sing in various high school groups under the urging of a pretty blue-eyed girl who was developing into an outstanding musician. Somehow, after an audition, I was selected to be a second tenor in the K-State Men's Glee Club, which meant my folks had to spring for the cost of a tuxedo.

Meanwhile my sister and I had our own rooms as we grew up. They were on the second floor and were very small with slanted ceilings that mimicked the roofline and on which I often bumped my head when getting up in the mornings. Between our rooms at the head of the narrow set of stairs was a small closet which we shared.

I even had a three- or four-foot high entrance to a small attic off my room. Somehow, my room stayed "warm enough" in the winter but miserably hot in the Kansas summertime heat.

I remember my Dad tacking plastic over the outside of our house's windows to help keep out the winter wind.

The house bordered a wheat field east of us and the railroad tracks ran within 75 or 100 yards of the vacant lot to the south. Like people who live near airports, the sound of locomotives and train whistles became so common and familiar that we took them for granted and eventually were not bothered by the noise – at least that's how I remember it. My folks and my sister might have different recollections.

I thought those railroad tracks must have led somewhere exciting and interesting. I don't recall riding a train, however, until I once made a trip home from college on one. As an elementary student, though, it was fun to walk east or west of town along the tracks and balance on the rails or step from one railroad tie to the next and not fear being crushed by a speeding train. Unlike the four young boys in the 1986 movie *Stand by Me* you could see miles down the track and there were no high bridges near Bushton so you could hear and see an oncoming train long before it was necessary to get off the tracks.

That kind of walk, out of town and into the "wilderness," was another form of freedom. I still have a couple of railroad spikes that I use for paperweights.

We had chickens. A vivid memory is of my Dad wringing the neck of a hen and watching it flop around the yard in its death throes before being plucked and cooked by my mother. The resulting fried chicken tasted wonderful as did almost everything my mother prepared (except perhaps anything containing okra or broccoli).

Lanara (Ostrander) Luthi ('58) has similar memories. "We raised chickens and butchered them every year," she said. "I can still visualize those headless chickens flopping around the alley. They, of course, had to be plucked (a smelly job) and Mom encouraged us to help. Then she dressed those naked birds. We were not allowed to help with this and I was glad. Another adult job was more smelly burning off of the pin feathers. This was a terrible chore but Mom cut up the chickens and we put them in a freezer we rented at the grocery store. By the time we started eating them they still tasted good." Like Lanara, I can still taste my mother's great fried chicken.

Linda and I painted the old chicken house.

    We had a chicken house in the backyard. Linda and I convinced my parents that it would make a wonderful clubhouse.

    Ultimately, painted in bright white on the green of the shed walls was "LLF&R Construction." That stood for **L**arry (me), **L**arry Anduss, **F**rancis Habiger and **R**obert Packer. We shared our toy construction trucks and related vehicles and had fun pretending to be construction engineers. Robert Packer, one of those who first welcomed me to town, was the "R." The second "L" - Larry Anduss - moved to Oklahoma and attended Oklahoma State University (known then as Oklahoma A&M). I later heard he became a radio announcer for OSU football games but got in trouble when he used a forbidden word on air when an athlete made a long gain. Francis Habiger ('56) was the "F" in the name of the fictional company and brother of Sue Habiger ('58), one of Ally's closest friends. Fran and Sue were the children of Ed and Louise Habiger, owners of a farm east of town a few miles from Ally's farm.

    Somehow, I still associate second-hand cigarette smoke with memories of that first Bushton house. Like many people in the '50s both my parents smoked – in the car, in the house, out for dinner and wherever else. After my Dad once passed out and the doctor blamed it on nicotine-caused "hardening of the arteries" they both quit. Around that same time the U.S. Surgeon General announced that smoking could cause cancer. Good for them for going through the agony of stopping.

    From a website -- https://healthtopquestions.com/newly-released-cancer-data -- I've learned that, while lung cancer, breast cancer, prostate cancer and colorectal cancer are the four leading causes of cancer-caused death, reducing new cases of cancer "greatly depends on tobacco control and the development of medical technology."

I smoked a pipe for several years, probably because I thought it made me look sophisticated, but I quit cold turkey when I ran out of pipe tobacco during a month-long consulting trip to China in the early 1990s. I haven't smoked since, except for a rare cigar with our son Greg. Even back in the '50s I knew my Dad had to quit smoking. The fact that both Mom and Dad quit together is a source of pride.

I revisited that "old" house years after we moved from it. At that time it was unused and trash littered every room. In my memories, and in actuality, my mother had kept it neat and spotless. I left quickly. I was astounded at how small it was.

Amor Towles, author of *A Gentleman in Moscow*, says if one has been absent for some time from a place he or she once loved, wise counsel would be that one should not return.

He cites examples in history of short-lived return visits to places of fond memory. Odysseus, for example, returned to Ithaca but left a few years later. And Robinson Crusoe, made it back to England but soon set sail for the very island where he had been stranded for so many years.

Towles suggests that a return can often spawn disappointment. The landscape may not be as wonderful, and one may find that, where he or she was once at the center of the world, he or she is now often barely recognized. The counsel he provides is to steer clear of the old homestead. But, he admits, that advice is not always suitable. Some may love returning to places that linger positively in their memory.

Late In the fifties we moved to a "new" house on the other side of the tracks. It wasn't much larger than the "old" one but it was newer and nicer. There were two bedrooms on the main floor (one for my parents and one for my sister). The house had a full basement and I had my room down there, next to my father's office. We still had a single-car detached garage but no vacant lot next door

The "new" house from the north side.

Another view of the "new" house with the Studebaker President in the driveway.

And one more view.

Not long ago I watched some home movies that pictured my Dad shoveling deep snow from the front sidewalk. My heart ached for him, for my Mom and sister, and for that house.

I have many memories of that house but one keeps leaping to the forefront of my thoughts. In that day *American Bandstand* was a popular television program among teenagers. One evening, Ally and I were in that house's basement dancing to a popular rock 'n roll song. Bravely, we tried a dance move we'd seen on TV but, as I tried to lift her upside down over my back I lost my grip and she slid to the side and banged her knee painfully on the concrete floor. My Dad had to come downstairs and apply some kind of liniment to her knee. As I recall, it embarrassed both of them terribly.

That was just like my Dad. He was a man's man but he had a soft side that cropped up when necessary. He was quiet and respectful. He could carry on a fine and engaging conversation in mixed company, treated my mother like a regal lady (which she was) and was polite and friendly to Ally. His grandkids would later love him dearly for his pleasant attitude and kindly nature toward them. He honestly loved them, too.

Ally and Dad

He could be tough when required. He worked among "roughnecks" in the oil fields, after all, and he could joke and get along with all of them. It seemed strange to me that he always wore a necktie and a nice hat (a fedora) even when working in the oil fields. He wore unbuckled galoshes to keep his shoes looking good and he kept his car clean and neat.

*Dad as a "lineman for the county" in Oklahoma.
That's him at the top in the center.*

    Dad was not tall but he carried himself as though he was. He could be tough when necessary such as when dealing with me over some infraction, even a minor one. But I knew he loved me. He enjoyed playing catch with me in the backyard and never missed a game in whatever sport I was involved in, at least as far as I can recall. I'm sure he treated my sister Linda the same. .

    Mom was as tall, and maybe taller, than him and she was just as tough. But she was definitely a lady. She disciplined Linda and me as necessary but we always knew she loved us dearly and that any discipline she laid on us was deserved and certainly didn't mean she loved us any less for it. She was beautiful and my Dad, now and then, would wonder "how the *&^% was I so lucky as to have her for a wife?"

    Looking back, I'm sure my Dad didn't make a great deal of money in those days but, somehow, he and Mom made sure my sister and I had what we needed, and some of the things we simply "wanted." Thanks folks.

    I'll never forget moving to Bushton and I'll never forget how important that town and her people were to me growing up.

* * * * *

Donnal Hiltbruner (Hoot) recalls that when he arrived in Bushton from Texas in January of 1951 he was in the middle of the 7th grade and it was what he termed "a unique experience."

He had never been in a classroom holding two different grades with one teacher. He remarked about "all the beautiful German names that sounded nothing like they were spelled, old timers who spoke with accents. No Hispanic or Black classmates. Becoming a 'Hoot' and losing my last name 'til senior graduation. Being a school janitor in the 8th grade. . . A beautiful blue-eyed bountiful blonde whose desk was behind me."

Hoot said "it was Shangri-la." It was, indeed, although I probably didn't think of it like that in 1951.

Those were carefree days and I don't recall being worried about much of anything. My parents, concerned though they might have been, never let on that there was anything I needed to worry about.

I now believe that attitude (thinking there was nothing I needed to worry about) was a definite black mark on my life's report card. Everything I did, I think now, was all about "me." I'm not sure I ever had a serious conversation with my parents during those years about "them." What did they want out of life? Were they happy? What did they think about the government and were they part of the political party in control at the time? Would they like to travel? If so, what countries would they like to visit? Would Dad like to re-visit some of the places where he fought in WWII?

What did they want of, or for, me?

Why didn't I have some serious conversations with my parents? I know why. I was concerned only with myself.

Maybe I was like most others of my age and, if so, and if that's the way all of us were, I'm disappointed and regretful that I concentrated so much on "me" and "mine" and ignored so much of "them" and "theirs."

I played with my buddies, rode my bike wherever I wanted, went to school and church, and, I guess, thought that's the way it would always be. Living in Bushton, it always seemed pretty much that way. Not for everyone, I know, but that's the way it was for me.

A sketch of the barn on the Groth family farm done by our son Greg on the 100th birthday of his grandfather Vernon Groth.

44 – **REAL, RURAL**

Chapter 2

What is Kansas?

Down a country road...

EXCEPT FOR THE OCCASIONAL swale or slight rise, the land in central Kansas is flat and boasts very few trees. Roads, for the most part, are as straight as the arrows that might have been used by the Kansa Indians who once roamed the Kansas plains, or as straight as a spear carried by a Spanish conquistador accompanying Don Francisco Vásquez de Coronado as he made his way across Kansas in the 16th Century during his unsuccessful search for the "Seven Cities of Gold."

A GoogleEarth Landsat photo of Bushton

on the plains of central Kansas.

Rows of cottonwood trees line the banks of the few creeks, and shelterbelts of trees and bushes create windbreaks that parallel many Kansas roads. Other than that, views are mostly unobstructed. That's just fine with most rural folks as anything else might block the incredible sight of a Kansas sunset that turns the western sky a fluorescent red and related pastel colors and helps one forget for a moment the freezing cold of winter or the intense summer heat that has baked the plains and leathered the faces of those who call the outdoors their office.

Being outdoors at the end of the day is a distinct pleasure for many of us. Author Beatriz Williams writes of a painter who loved the final hour of the day because the light gave inspiring clarity to the world. He called it "the golden hour." I agree. In Kansas, as the sun pauses on the rim of the earth it casts long shadows across the land and illuminates the prairie with deep colors and glorious rich tones unseen during the harshness of full daylight. A lone tree, for example, windblown and battered by the contrasts of seasonal weather, takes on a beauty unique to the plains.

Author Truman Capote writes of the land in his 1965 true crime book *In Cold Blood.*

The land is flat, he says, and the views are awesomely extensive. He sees horses and herds of cattle and describes a

*The grain elevator is a welcoming sight
as one enters Bushton from the north.*

white cluster of grain elevators rising as gracefully as Greek temples which are visible long before a traveler reaches them.

There are certain smells and textures that remind me clearly of my youth in Rice County Kansas. The soil is, for the most part, black and fertile. It has, naturally, an earthy smell all its own that emanates from deep within the continent and speaks of legions of insects and animals that roamed and died there and whose decayed carcasses fertilized the ground and prepared it layer-by-layer for the many world-feeding millennia that would make mid-America ultimately famous as a breadbasket.

Many of those same insects and animals were important to the formation of vast pools of oil that developed quietly far beneath the fertile topsoil over much the same millennia and provided another means of livelihood for those who recognized its worth. The smell of oil from ubiquitous oil wells, pumping units and drilling rigs was not especially pleasant but we claimed it "smelled like money."

The odor from what is referred to as the Central Kansas Uplift is one of the defining features one notes when driving through the area. Active, pumping oil wells appear in clusters of several or as alone as a wandering cow in a large pasture. Thank God for the oil. It is what brought my Dad to Bushton.

The top oil-producing county in Kansas is only two counties to the northwest of Rice County. Ellis County produced 260,000,000 barrels of oil in 2018, the most recent year for which figures were available as this was written. Rice County was in the third tier of oil-producing counties with 624,000 barrels. The three top counties behind Ellis County are all adjacent, or nearly so, to Rice County. They are Barton (169,200,000), Russell (155,800,000) and Stafford (101,900,000).

The Central Kansas Uplift, by the way, is a structural feature running northwest and southeast across west-central Kansas which originated in pre-Cambrian time and which has a geologic history similar to that of the Ozarks of Missouri.

It seems as though all the land is or has been cultivated. It's a combination of hard baseball-sized clods of brown dirt that turn a healthy looking black after a rain, and fine broken-up soil that weighs about as much as a baseball in one's hand. Some of the land is irrigated. Much of it is not and optimistic farmers avoid draining more of the Ogallala Aquifer and pray for rain.

Some of the land is virgin and thankfully retains the prairie look that our ancestors first laid eyes on when they arrived from some distant shore. There was a small piece of the farm where Ally grew up that remained untouched by plow or disk.

It reminds me of a line from William Least Heat-Moon's popular book about central Kansas called *PrairyErth*. Least Heat-Moon is the author of *Blue Highways*. A college student from Pennsylvania who was working on a ranch near the small town of Matfield Green said to Least Heat-Moon: "I can't believe this. I can't believe it's still like this. I mean, it's so Americana."

Walter Prescott Webb, a pre-eminent American historian, describes the plains states in his 1931 book The Great Plains. This has become a classic picture of the people of that area of the county as well as a description of the plains, its geologic evolution, and the changes it has undergone through the millennia. Webb declares that practically every idea, person or institution that entered the Great Plains was almost always broken and remade or at least in many ways greatly changed.

To me, that patch of undisturbed land on Ally's farm looked like the middle-America of long ago as described by Webb. It also smelled of those ancient days and the animals that once grazed there.

Wheatfields, by the way, smell of dust and wind-blown chaff from a combine's discharge of grains of golden wheat.

Oats itch.

Haybales smell of dirt and weeds and a pungent bite of rich farmland.

Chicken coops smell terrible.

Pigpens are worse.

Pastures where cattle graze smell of rich manure and resonate with the sounds of bawling cattle telling everyone, maybe especially their calves, where they are.

And always, the Kansas wind brings those smells, and more, to the nostrils of one who is attuned to such things. By the way, as most Kansans know, Kansas is named for "the people of the south wind" – the Kansa Indians. The wind is seemingly constant, usually strong and always hot or cold, depending on the season. It wouldn't be Kansas without it.

Likewise, when I run my hand over the bark of a rough cottonwood tree or grab a small branch of a young willow and use it like a rope to help me up a steep creekbank I am reminded of Kansas trees. The strength of those few trees sprouting up and out of the harsh and dry prairie is mirrored by the tough Kansas farmers who weathered, and continue to weather, heat and cold, drought and flood, wind and dust to conquer the plains.

The land is a "constant" that I recall about living in Rice County. Like those who farmed it or drilled into it, I depended on it. It was always there. A certain gravel road would always take me to the same place, time after time. A lone cottonwood tree was a landmark. A streambed, often dry or sometimes barely a trickle, could be counted on to appear where it always had. Wheat would cover a vast acreage of land year-after-year.

It was the land that made us rural. It was the land that sustained us and gave us life. The land was everything and it was beautiful and ugly and smelly and dirty and productive and barren and, yes, flat. One could see across it to more land. Good land. God-given land.

* * * *

A book called *The Atlas of the New West* published by the Center of the American West at the University of Colorado, Boulder, in 1997, identifies the "new west" (as opposed to the "old west," I suppose) as beginning at the Front Range of the Rocky Mountains and excluding most of the west coast. California, for example, is not included in the New West. I assume that might be because the editors considered California almost a "separate country."

The point being, Kansas, though acknowledged to be a part of the "Wild" West, is not included in the "New" West.

The New West, the editors of this book say, officially began in 1972 when voters in Colorado passed a ballot measure by a hefty 3-2 margin, barring the state from spending any funds on the Olympic Games which had been proposed for Colorado.

The editors say the creation of Vail, the rise of a high-stakes recreation industry, and the dispute over the Olympics epitomized a new dynamic in the region.

Horan and Sann say the Wild West was a time as well as a place. In *A Pictorial History of the Wild West* they describe the place as roughly from the border of Kansas and Missouri to the Pacific Ocean. The time, they say, was roughly from the end of the Civil War to the turn of the century.

Shoot. Despite what the authors of *The Atlas of the New West* say. I thought we'd stay a part of the Wild West and be included in the New West. After all, the Santa Fe Trail crossed Kansas and has found a place in history for its pioneering trading of goods far from what was then considered "civilization." A portion of that famous trail, I've since learned, passed not far from the ultimate site of Bushton and left much evidence of its passing at various camping spots and, for example, what are known as "Ralph's Ruts," named for a farmer near Lyons across whose land the trail ran. There are remaining wagon wheel ruts elsewhere but Ralph's seem the most famous.

I've known all along, perhaps because I still want to be a cowboy when I grow up, that Kansas was a part of the Wild West. The raucous cowtowns of Dodge City, Hays, Abilene, Ellsworth and other such towns are part of the lore of cowboys and cattle drives and shootouts and some of the West's most famous outlaws and lawmen.

I've since also learned that the era of the great cattle drives into Kansas ended only a couple of years before the founding of Bushton. At that time the Kansas Legislature, alarmed by the increase of the cattle disease called "Texas Fever' brought into the state by the Texas tick, passed legislation forbidding the importation of Texas cattle between March 1 and December 1, the historic season for the long drives.

Among the significant trails, the Chisholm Trail to Ellsworth came nearest to where Bushton would be founded only a few years later. It later branched off to Abilene as the railroad moved farther east. Also included was the Western Trail to Dodge City and on north to Ogallala, Nebraska, and the Sedalia and Baxter Springs Trail to Baxter Springs in southeastern

Kansas which later branched off to Sedalia, Missouri.

Not long before that the last Indian battle in Kansas took place on the bluffs of Ladder Creek, now Beaver Creek, just south of Scott City in western Kansas. Chiefs Dull Knife and Little Wolf of the Northern Cheyenne, while leading their people in a rebellion and flight from confinement and starvation on a reservation in Indian Territory (now the state of Oklahoma), made their final stand against the U.S. Cavalry in September of 1878.

I did know, perhaps because I lived in a farming community that Mennonites from Russia had introduced Turkey Red Wheat to Kansas, and that German Catholics (Volga Germans) who also emigrated from Russia had founded several small towns in Kansas. The towns have names such as Catherine, Munjor, Pfeifer, Schoenchen and Liebenthal.

I have been reminded that in 1880 an amendment to the Kansas Constitution approved by Kansas voters prohibited the manufacture, sale or gift of all forms of intoxicating liquor. Kansas became the first state in the United States to pass this controversial amendment.

I was also interested to learn that Carry Nation had lived in Medicine Lodge, Kansas, before she began her crusade against liquor that took her across the United States and as far away as England.

Just as interesting, and something that I don't recall learning in high school, was the fact that in 1887, the year of Bushton's founding, Susanna Medoro Salter of Argonia, Kansas, became the first woman in the U.S. to be elected a mayor.

By the time Bushton was founded almost all the buffalo that had once dominated the state were gone. However, Ally knows that buffalo once roamed her family's farm and cites what she calls a "mysterious" buffalo wallow in her south pasture as "clear evidence."

In *The Destruction of the Bison*, Andrew C. Isenberg discusses the decline of the North American bison population from an estimated 30 million in 1800 to fewer than 1000 a century later. He believes that the encounter between Native Americans and Euroamericans in the Great Plains was the cause of the near-extinction of the bison. He also believes that nostalgia about the bison, ironically became an important impetus to its preservation.

Maybe we were taught all or most of that in Bushton. I simply don't remember it. Perhaps I simply wasn't paying attention.

I still want to be a cowboy when I grow up.

Chapter 3

Immigrants All

Down a country road...

MANY OF THOSE WHOSE sweat has dripped onto parched Kansas soil have names that resonate of faraway places and exotic-sounding homelands.

Ally's maiden name was Groth, shortened from Von Groth at the time of the First World War, long after her ancestors had emigrated to the U.S. from Prussia which was essentially the birthplace of modern Germany.

My name, Meredith, is Welsh, a derivative of Maredudd or Meredydd, possibly meaning "great lord" or "sea lord."

In central Kansas we were far from any "sea." However, we were not the only families with names extracted from countries throughout the world. There were, in no particular order, folks with names like Behnke, Poppelreiter, Muth, Schmitt, Volkland, Ostrander, Nordstrom, Schroeder, Habiger, Roelfs, Loutzenhiser, Schwerdtfeger and many others. As far as I can recall we didn't have anyone named Jones or O'Hara, for example. And, frankly, a name like Heinz or Oberle or Teghtmeyer didn't seem especially strange to the students of the Bushton schools. Nor did the names of many of the nearby small towns such as Zook, Dundee, Milberger, Holyrood, Otis, Bison or Timken.

Kansas and neighboring states were settled, after all, mainly by immigrants who came into the heartland on ever-expanding railroads during the quest for a transcontinental route. States and the Federal Government gave funds and made land grants to the railroads which built towns every few miles along their routes to assure there would be passengers and freight and to support the farmers who populated the plains.

An early photo of Bushton scanned from a postcard. The date is smudged but it appears to be "1909."

Often, there is confusion regarding the difference between immigrant and emigrant. For those who are interested, here's the way to differentiate: If you are an Italian citizen, for example, and moving out of the country to settle in the US, you are an emigrant for all your friends and relatives back in Italy. In fact, to all those who reside within Italian boundaries, you will be labeled as an emigrant. But, for those in the US, you are an immigrant. That is because you have come from another country to settle in their country. So, for US people, you are an immigrant.

In his 1996 book *Bad Land: An American Romance* (published by Vintage Books), author Jonathan Raban writes that as the railroads advanced across the lands, they planted infant cities at intervals of a dozen miles or so. Trains needed to carry freight and passengers, and it was part of the business of the railroad to furnish its territory with customers. So the company built these market centers on company-owned land. Its creations were as arbitrary as those described in Genesis and, like a God, when they said let there be a city there was a city.

Bushton was one of those towns created by the railroad. The name was originally *Sorghum* when it was established in the early 1880s. It was renamed Bushton in 1887, according to several sources, after the number of wild bushes (probably plum bushes, Ally says) growing at the town site. The town was incorporated in 1907.

During the 19th Century more than a million square miles of land west of the Mississippi River was acquired by the U.S.

Government. This led to widespread migration west, referred to as Westward Expansion.

"Manifest Destiny" was the belief that it was settlers' God-given right to claim the entire North American continent. The notion of Manifest Destiny was why European settlers felt they had a right to claim land, both inhabited and uninhabited, in western North America. They believed it was the white man's destiny to prosper and spread Christianity by claiming and controlling land.

The fiftieth anniversary publication for the town of Bushton in 1937 (Thanks to Dale Nordstrom)

Manifest Destiny was also used to validate the "Indian Removal Acts" which occurred in the 1830s. Such legislation forced the removal of Native Americans and helped clear the way for non-native settlers to claim land in the west. When the settlers reached land populated or previously promised to Native Americans, they had no qualms about claiming it for their own benefit.

Native Americans, rightly or wrongly, were often blamed for the slow advancement of railroads across the plains and, rightly or wrongly, the U.S. military was dispatched to deal with the "war-mongering" Indians. Stephen E. Ambrose, author of *Crazy Horse and Custer* explains that at this time George Armstrong Custer was stationed in Kansas and roamed across the state. A Lieutenant-Colonel in the Seventh Cavalry at the time,

Custer was described by General John Sherman as young and very brave.

Ambrose said General Winfield Scott Hancock, commanding the Department of the Missouri and stationed at Fort Leavenworth in Kansas, was sent on a grand campaign to clear the Indians out of Kansas and Nebraska. Custer would lead the way.

The trouble, Ambrose says, was that neither Hancock nor Custer knew anything about Indians or about the Plains, while they both had an exaggerated idea of their own abilities.

The expedition set out on March 22, 1867, twenty years before Bushton was founded.

It was the clear duty of the Army at that time to protect the advancing frontier and the transcontinental railroads, and the Indians *were* in the way. They had to be removed if the nation's destiny was to be realized. And in view of the expanding white population, and the growing world demand for foodstuffs the prevailing thought was that the red men could not be allowed to retain hundreds of square miles of prime grazing or wheat country in order to support a few thousand Indians.

The increasing number of settlers coming into Kansas in the 19th Century was due to one of the most comprehensive advertising campaigns the nation had ever known. The campaign was planned and executed by the railroads and soon the promotion of immigration and the development of towns became an important and accepted part of railroad activity. To counteract the association of the word "Kansas" in the minds of easterners with grasshoppers, drought and starvation, the railroads advertised the state as a literal paradise. Advertisements, posters and pamphlets promoted Kansas and the West to potential immigrants throughout the world.

Most of the readers of those ads, posters and pamphlets had no real idea of Kansas. In those days, coming to America was a journey to a foreign land of extraordinary largesse and a lot of strange niceties. There were second helpings there, immigrants were told, and cups and saucers, and houses were often loud with the talk of grown-up visitors all dressed up in neckties and cravats, long skirts and starched white blouses.

There may have been town families or those who populated farms who grandly dressed up like that but, if so, I didn't know them. Bushton's Centennial publication, published in 1987, describes a different kind of family:

"Most settlers gathered corn stalks and pulled corn stubs to burn" for warmth, the publication states. "Rags were braided and put in a saucer of grease and then lit for a light. Few people had cows because they were so expensive, but the few in town were confined near the houses by tying ropes to their horns and staking the rope in the ground. A buggy was a sight for sore eyes. Horses were scarce. Grasshoppers were numerous at times and destroyed many crops."

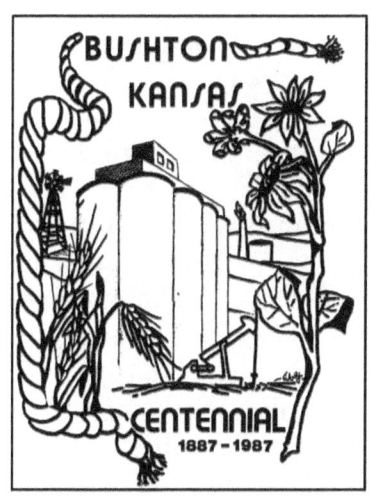

The cover of the Bushton Centennial publication from 1987

Two of the first buildings erected in the new little towns were a school and a church. "Most of the students attended school barefooted and were quite humbly dressed," the Centennial publication says.

To many (but not all) of the people in Bushton during the '50s, rural America was, indeed, as the railroad's pamphlets promised, a paradise.

* * * *

In 1957, when the graduating class totaled 12, there were 88 students enrolled in the high school but 179 in grades K through 8. The town might have seemed to be growing but, alas, many of those students came in from nearby farms.

Alyce Lyn Groth (Ally) was one of those who rode a "bus" to school from her folks' farm five miles east of town on old Highway 4. We were lucky. We found each other as youngsters and have lived a wonderful life for many years. We have two children and two grandchildren. That's plenty. Our parents adored our kids and were adored by them.

Growing up rural was no big deal to either of us. It was simply the way it was in our families and as natural as the sun coming up already blazing hot in the summer and shining beautifully over the fields of wheat or, in the cold heart of winter, hardly warming the white landscape and sending glittering sparkles across the snow which was protecting the winter wheat and preparing it for growing green and then golden in the spring and summer.

Ally's Prussian ancestors had settled on farms in central and southwestern Kansas. Whether they purchased their farms or if they somehow homesteaded them is unclear. But early in the 20th Century, when Teddy Roosevelt was President, his administration forcefully backed the homesteading of the dry West. From his viewpoint homesteading would "relieve the pressure on the overcrowded cities." This was a time when America feared it might soon be unable to feed itself and homesteading dry-land farmers would enlarge the wheat belt. And more farmers also meant more cattle.

In 1909 Roosevelt's *Commission on Country Life* delivered its report to the Senate. The report said rural society in the U.S. was in a "bad way" and "much of the fault lay in the inherent character of the American farmer." The report said, of the farmer, "self-reliance being the essence of his nature, he does not at once feel the need of cooperation for business purposes or of close association for social objects." In other words, the farmer does not easily play well with others (my words). He is a strong individualist who has been obliged to rely mainly on himself.

The report was clear in saying "it is the government's

responsibility to socialize and educate the farmer, to bring him into line with his well-drilled, well-ordered fellow citizens in the suburbs." Rural, state and federal agencies needed to be strengthened, the report said, "in order to subdue the crew of tousle-headed individualists working on the land." It said inspectors needed to be appointed, to see that official standards were being met in "herds, barns, crops, orchards and farms."

At the beginning of Richard Rhodes' 1989 book *Farm: A Year in the Life of an American Farmer*, he quotes J. Hector St. John de Crevecoeur, author of *Thoughts of an American Farmer on Various Rural Subjects* published in 1782.

In the 18th Century, the quote says: "the philosopher's stone of an American farmer is to do everything within his own family, to trouble his neighbors by borrowing as little as possible, and to abstain from buying European commodities. He that follows that golden rule and has a good wife is almost sure of succeeding."

The author Richard Rhodes and I shared an office at Hallmark Cards in Kansas City for two years. Dick's book *The Making of the Atomic Bomb* won the Pulitzer Prize and the National Book Award in 1987 and also the National Book Critics Circle Award.

Meanwhile, early in the century, about the time the report of the *Commission on Country Life* came out, Extension Agents were sent to the West to assure that the "finger of government should be firmly planted in every pie." This, like the report of the Commission, ran hard against the grain of American cultural tradition. These Extension Agents, who seemed to farmers in Kansas and elsewhere like a swarm of locusts, were not welcomed enthusiastically, if at all.

The Groth family farm five miles east of Bushton where Ally grew up.

One of the messages they brought was that the "country church needed to be reorganized" to "counter the dangerous tide of both rural irreligion and the growth of narrow and divisive sects and cults." Everywhere, these Agents and the Commission found "evidence of an uncorrelated and unadjusted society" and "not nearly enough obedient and forward-thinking citizens" (meaning, I think, city folk).

One of the final straws might have been when the Extension Agents settled on the theme of the need for shelterbelts of trees and at least one Agent remarked that "those who had never lived anywhere else couldn't appreciate the value of trees."

At the time, that idea didn't get very far, perhaps due to the natural distrust of anyone from the East on the part of these "individualistic" farmers. However, the Agents, as it turned out, had a point but it was made years too soon. Shelterbelts are now a plentiful and easily visible impediment to the constant wind in the central plains.

Some continue to insist that the federal response to the Dust Bowl, including the Prairie States Forestry project which planted the Great Plains Shelterbelt and created the Soil Erosion Service represents the "largest and most-focused effort of the [U.S.] government to address an environmental problem."

Nevertheless, Washington's intrusion on the domain of the dry-land farmer in the early 1900s was unwelcome and not much has changed in that regard.

Ally's father Vernon never said anything, at least in my presence, regarding how he felt about government's influence on farming in Kansas. He graduated from Bushton High School in 1930 and lived on his Rice County Kansas farm his entire life except for a few years when he attended and graduated from Sterling College, a small Presbyterian-related school in Sterling, Kansas, barely 30 miles from the farm.

Interestingly, Vernon majored in music at Sterling and brought his degree back to the farm with a brand new wife, Leola (nee McCreight), who had been an X-ray technician in Dr. Trueheart's office in Sterling. She had managed to have many of her lunches in the Sterling College cafeteria where she caught Vernon's eye. They were married for 69 years before Leola died in 2005. Vernon, a music-loving wheat and cattle farmer who often worked part-time as a banker, was born in 1912, died in 2014 and lived to within two months of being 102 years old.

The Bushton High basketball team of 1930. Ally's father Vernon is holding the basketball in the front row.

Leola and Vernon Groth

My parents, Lawrence and Eva (both from Oklahoma), were married for 55 years before my father died in August of 1990 of a combination of Parkinson's and pneumonia just prior to turning 80. My mother died in March of 2003. Neither of them had much education. Dad was a small man but tough. I've got a photo of him with his high school football team and he looks like an aggressive lineman who could easily intimidate the opposition. Like Ally's folks, my mom and dad grew up and were married during the years of the Great Depression. Both came from large families and because of that I've got aunts and uncles and cousins, buried and alive, scattered throughout the country. I think I know the names of all of them.

Eva and Lawrence Meredith

My Mom was a strong woman who took the hardships of life along with the good times. After my Dad died she lived alone for more than a decade and was almost blind with glaucoma. My sister and I blame that on an optometrist (maybe he was an ophthalmologist) who didn't diagnose the problem soon enough and, when he finally did, failed to treat it properly. At any rate, my Mom had very narrow tunnel vision, listened to audio renditions of countless books, and kept up with national and local news. Once, when my sister Linda had just finished helping her move into a senior living facility in Wichita, Mom refused Linda's aid in finding her way to the dining room and getting acquainted. She wanted to do it herself, nearly blind as she was. And she did.

My Dad was also tough. As a young man he worked at various jobs in Oklahoma and Arkansas, often for less than $1 a day. When he was in his early 30s he was drafted into the Army (even though he was married and had two children). He served well (including a stint in the Battle of the Bulge) and came home to us safe and eager to return to civilian life.

My Dad in the military   *Dad at Atlas Supply in Russell*

Early in his married life Dad began selling oil field equipment for Atlas Supply (later it became Jones and Laughlin Supply Co.) and, because he was involved in the oil fields of Oklahoma and Kansas, was frequently transferred to small communities. The company sent him to Bushton when I was in the 4th grade and we were able to stay there until my sister, Linda, and I went away to college.

    This was especially fortunate because Ally and I were in the process of falling in love and planning a future together. That's what was on our minds in those days, not Bushton's history or, for that matter, even very much of what went on in Kansas "back in the day."

CHAPTER 4

An "adequate" Education

Down a country road...

WE KNEW THERE WERE salt mines in and around Hutchinson, a town located roughly 40 miles southeast of Bushton with a population of maybe 35,000 in the mid-1950s. But I don't recall ever being taught the fact that in 1887, the year my town of Bushton was founded, a man named Sam Blanchard struck salt at 300 feet while drilling a well. The town of Hutchinson had been built on top of one of the **world's greatest salt deposits**. Within a year, I've since learned, there were nearly a dozen salt plants in operation in or around the city.

My class toured the Hutchinson salt mines in 1952 thanks to our elementary school principal Lawrence Timmons. At that time we very likely were told how that salt got there. If so, I don't remember it. I've only recently found the answer.

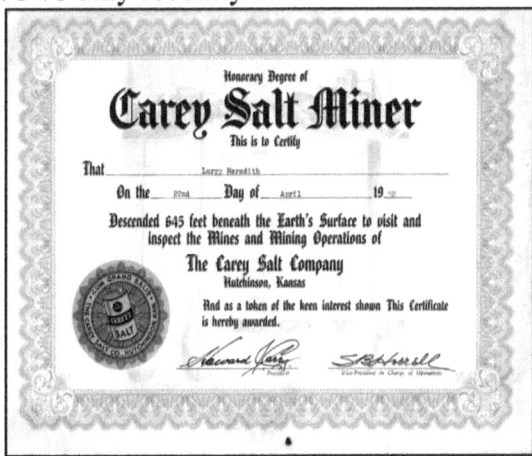

Proof that I toured the Salt Mine in 1952.

I don't want to demean the quality of the education (through high school) I received in Bushton because I did as well or better in college than some others in my classes when I started at K-State as a freshman in 1957. However, like most folks, I've learned a lot since then that was not a part of the high school curriculum. I keep reminding myself that I was a liberal arts student in college so didn't need all the scientific and technical knowledge that was required of some others, including my brother-in-law, Wayne Groth ('61), who earned an engineering degree from K-State in '65 and made a career of it.

Dale Nordstrom ('55) also had a career as an engineer after graduating from K-State and has a take different from mine on the education he received in Bushton. Dale called it an "adequate" education and said "it wasn't until I went to Boys State in Wichita and college in Manhattan that I realized how much I had missed." Others disagree and often remark that, thanks to the increasing taxes from a thriving oil industry in and around the town, and a Northern Natural Gas Company booster station constructed just northeast of town, Bushton's education system was better than that of some neighboring towns and appropriate for our later lives. But there are some who shared Dale Nordstrom's concerns.

Darrol Timmons ('58), for example, studied Nuclear Engineering at K-State and found that while some of his high school education was excellent – "English thanks to Miss Holland and Chemistry, thanks to Mr. Tiner" – he rated other courses "either adequate or lacking." Timmons discovered that "classmates from larger schools had a much better background" than he had in certain areas. Consequently, he had to learn some of the basics that the college professors expected freshman students to have coming into class. "I was even further behind in physics," he said, because the high school course was scheduled at the same time as U.S. history with no option for rescheduling either. History was required for graduation. Physics was, by necessity, often bypassed. "Those were the only disadvantages I experienced from having attended a small high school," he concluded.

Wayne Groth's view varied just a little from Nordstrom's

and Timmons'. "Most everyone had a teacher who provided a spark and introduced a new concept that opened up a new world of possibilities," he said. "I had that in a chemistry and math teacher who challenged me." He said that same teacher gave him the direction to pursue a career that used those disciplines.

Darrol Timmons offered a positive recollection involving one of his favorite teachers who was also one of mine, Jim Tiner. "I had a study hall during the period just before Chemistry," Darrol said, "and Mr. Tiner was the study hall monitor." When Darrol told him he planned to enroll in the Nuclear Option of Chemical Engineering at K-State Mr. Tiner allowed him to cut study hall and set up the demonstration experiment he would be using during the next class in chemistry. To do so properly Darrol had to study and understand the teacher's manual. "I believe I learned more from the teacher's manual than from the textbook," he said.

Jim Tiner, (photo scanned from the yearbook)

However, Neil Denton, a National Merit Scholar and good friend whom I followed to K-State and the Sigma Chi fraternity, says he earned his scholarship "in spite of the education" he received in the Bushton schools.

As for me, I muddled through high school and, in college, was more interested in writing for the K-State daily newspaper, the *Collegian,* than in studying for my other classes which included, for example "U.S. Since 1865," "Modern Democracy" or "French." I did well enough to make my grades and become an active Sigma Chi fraternity member, to stay enrolled and to finally graduate.

Ally, on the other hand, graduated from the University of Wichita Cum Laude.

Neil Denton and me being polite for the cameraman in the 1950s.

Before I graduated from high school my Uncle Bill (H.G. Williams, my Mom's brother) learned of an association in Tulsa, Oklahoma, that offered aptitude testing for young people like me. Their success rate was very good as they compared interests, skills and academic subjects of practicing professionals in many fields with those of high schoolers and suggested potential career paths for students. My uncle, who was very successful as a businessman in Wichita, paid for my testing. Of the many careers that were suggested to me were those of a minister of the gospel and a journalist. I forgot about my early thinking that I would go into dentistry and opted for journalism. It was a wonderful decision that I've never regretted. Incidentally, my sister Linda was afforded that same opportunity by Uncle Bill but I don't know where she was directed as a career. Anyway, she met one of my good friends and fraternity brothers at K-State during her freshman year and she and Bob Byers were married soon after that. I take great credit in having introduced them.

*Bob and Linda
(my sister) Byers*

As I got into my first year or two of college I began to think seriously about my rural background. K-State was a Land Grant College that was initially Kansas State Agricultural College with a reputation of attracting students from smaller towns and cities in the central and western areas of the state. The university is today classified as one of 115 research universities with highest research activity (R1) by the Carnegie Classification of Institutions of Higher Education and, since 1986, K-State ranks first nationally among public universities in its total of Rhodes, Marshall, Truman, Goldwater, and Udall scholars with 124 recipients. Those achievements were primarily earned after I received my BA degree but evidence of early commitment to high academic standards was even then somewhat daunting.

For the first time I began to question my high school education. Was it strong enough to allow me to compete evenly with students from larger schools? Were the courses I took in high school the right ones in preparation for college work?

Was I attending what students at the University of Kansas, our main rival, called a "cow college" and would a degree from there be what I needed to find success in some as yet unknown job out in the "real" world? (As an insert here, while KU students called us "Silo Tech" we said KU students were attending "Snob Hill.")

It was the first time I had, in my own mind, called into question the quality of education I received in high school. As it turned out, I did just fine – not great, but just fine – despite what some would consider an education that was barely adequate.

The 1950s Bushton School. Elementary School on right, high school on left, gym in the center.

Dale Nordstrom recalled that in high school emphasis was on "science, history, proper English, shop class for the boys and home economics for the girls. Teaching reading, writing and arithmetic were the primary goals in elementary school."

In the 20th Century the schoolhouse was often an emblem of the fact that people were here for keeps. The amount of education a family's children (boy or girl) would receive depended largely on the attitude of the father. In Bushton, the school was at the center of all that was good and, even though it was a legal requirement that youngsters attend school, most parents saw its value. However, as even today, some important elements of a complete education were missing.

For example, Randall J. Condon was Superintendent of the Cincinnati Schools and general editor of the Atlantic Readers series. In the foreword of Condon's schoolbooks he writes much about "nationalism" but it turns out, in practice, to be a simple pride in America for having gathered so many traditions under one flag and for incorporating so many beautiful landscapes in one political geography. Native Americans are treated well; black Americans are not mentioned – any recognition of them would have been hard to square with Condon's expressed dream of racial equality for all.

In Bushton, some students believed that, from their perspective there was little effort to expose students to the fine arts like classical music and great artists."

My wife Ally disagrees. Thanks in large part to her parents and to a music instructor named Lyle Meredith (no relation) she delved deeply into the fine arts and became an outstanding pianist and vocalist with a degree in Music from the

University of Wichita (now Wichita State University). At her graduation ceremony from WSU she performed a Saint-Saëns piano concerto with the college symphony.

While earning his degree in music from Sterling College her father Vernon sang in the college quartet and toured the state with the group giving concerts in schools and churches wherever possible. Ally's mother was a fine pianist in her own right and "good" music echoed throughout their farm home from their piano or from a record player for much of every day. Ally was exposed to a love of music that went beyond the early days of Rock 'n Roll to include classical and religious compositions. As a high school senior she sang a one-act opera, *The Telephone* or *L'Amour a trois* by Gian Carlo Menotti with Lyle Meredith to a large crowd. She has since taught elementary music, performed with orchestras and as a soloist, has been the pianist for several churches, formed and led several handbell choirs in churches, and served as collaborative pianist for the Western Colorado University Music Department in Gunnison, accompanying various musical groups and individuals and helping young musicians along with their careers. She said her parents made special efforts to take her to Community Concerts in Lyons and Great Bend and to other musical events, "and hauled me everywhere for piano lessons and music competitions." She said she has been directed professionally "by being surrounded by a family with a love of music. And I have inherited those genes."

It's interesting to note that, as Ivan Doig recalls in the novel Work Song, a great man once said "mankind's two great magics are words and music." Does anyone know who to credit with that quote? I've been unable to find out.

Ally at the piano

As an aside, our family members all seem to be "right brained." None of us excel in math or science. Ally and our daughter Suzy Meredith-Orr are both outstanding musicians while our son (Greg) is a fine artist with a degree in Art from Western Colorado University in Gunnison. And I'm something of a writer. Go figure. Suzy attended the Conservatory of Music at the University of Missouri in Kansas City.

Suzy Meredith-Orr

Greg Meredith

I believe Ally's experience, and that of others, illustrates my belief that the quality of education one receives depends, in large part, on how the individual reacts to teaching, how the student is motivated by parents or other role models and the desire within each student to learn and achieve.

Myretta (Behnke) Bell ('58) insists there was "culture" in Bushton. "Our little school presented operettas," she said. "In first or second grade I was one of the Northern Lights in Humperdinck's *Hansel and Gretel*. Somewhere I have the photo Effie Volkland took."

Dale Nordstrom said "I suspect that everyone you talk to

who attended school in Bushton has a different perspective" and that is certainly the case. Dale admits that he was not highly motivated and just coasted through school. "I paid the piper in college," he said. "I see what I was exposed to and what kids today are exposed to (education-wise) and it's like night and day."

He admits that this isn't a fair comparison. "Times were different," he said, "but there was a limited view of the country and the world in Bushton." Dale admits that much of what he missed was his own fault, not the teachers. "I concentrated on today, not tomorrow," he said. (Many of us did the same.) "All that being said, there were a lot of graduates from Bushton schools who have been successful in life."

I agree with Dale in that previous thought. Among those I know who completed high school within a few years of my own graduation, before and after, I can name doctors, engineers, college professors, decorated military officers, teachers, musicians, authors, newspaper editors, businessmen and women, farmers and livestock producers and leaders in many other professions.

Many agree. Myretta, who finished high school in Hutchinson in 1958 after her grandfather died, is one of them. Myretta went to Hutchinson to live with, and help care for, her widowed grandmother. Still, she maintained a love for Bushton. "From our little burg there appeared to be an inordinate number of professional careers in business and medical fields represented," she said.

My classmate Mildred Dundas believes Bushton had a good school system with many good teachers. "Many of our classmates have had very successful careers," she said.

Likewise, Joy Nickerson said "the school was small but did a good job of turning out students ready to go on to college or take a job."

Personally, I have to give our wonderful English teacher Miss Willa Holland ("Banty") a great deal of credit for my ultimate interest in reading and writing.

Miss Holland found and recommended reading material for me. Most of those books came from the school's meagre library. I read Richard Halliburton's *Royal Road to Romance* more than once and carried it around with my hand covering the title. The book was about Halliburton's travel adventures around the world but I didn't want my classmates seeing the title and thinking it was about something else. It was published in 1925.

Mom, bless her heart, was a willing accomplice to Miss Holland. She never overtly encouraged or urged me to read but often, I believe to this day, brought books home from the library or a bookstore, and left them lying around the house hoping, I am sure, that I would discover and read them. I did.

Thanks Mom.

Sue Dahlsten recalls some fun memories of high school in Bushton which, she said, "had one coach and one principal and no secretary." Sue and Ally were good friends and Sue recalled once when the two of them got "kicked out of algebra or geometry" and sent to the principal's office. "No one was there," she said, "so we got to visit and even answer the phone." Sue remembered that when her parents asked Principal Arthur Harvey why she got removed from class, he said, "Oh, I don't want the other students to think I am favoring Sue and Alyce because their dads are on the school board so I just do it for show." Sue's parents were not pleased and said they wanted her in class "so that was the end of our fun."

Nevertheless, she exclaimed about "how wonderful those times were" and she cherishes them. "I'm so glad we had respect for our parents, teachers, pastors and friends," she said.

Don "Hoot" Hiltbrunner, a Marine Corps aviator who saw action during the Vietnam War and attained the rank of Colonel, is effusive in praise of the school. "Our school molded us and instilled us with life skills by teachers that are forever imprinted on our lives," he said. "Graduates truly knew the meaning of duty (do your job), honor (citizenship), country (respect the constitution and 10 Commandments) as they matured into their profession. They were the salt of the earth." Hoot said the "far reaching accomplishments and successes" of many Bushton graduates have "greatly contributed to our country." He said "enough cannot be said about what a remarkable asset Bushton Rural High School was to our nation."

Hiltbrunner earned several medals including the Silver Star, Purple Heart, Air Medal (16th AWD), Navy Commendation Medal with Combat "V", National Defense Service Medal (2nd Award), Presidential Unit Citation, Navy Unit Commendation (2nd Award), Joint Services Commendation Medal, Republic of Vietnam Meritorious Unit Citation (Gallantry Cross Color with Palm), Republic of Vietnam Meritorious Unit Citation (Civil Action, 1st Class Color with Palm), Republic of Vietnam Commendation Media, Meritorious Service Medal, Vietnam Service Medal and Sea Service Deployment Ribbon.

Sue Dahlsten related a story that only slightly relates to education, but that is interesting in its own right. "The girls all had to wear skirts or dresses to school," she said, "except on Fridays when I believe we could wear jeans. No shorts were allowed." She said one time some of her group decided to wear Bermuda shorts. "That didn't go over too well," she said, "and we were sent home to change." A sign of the times?

At least to a degree, I must agree with Dale Nordstrom and Darrol Timmons. For example, we learned very little (that's true for me, at least) about the history, geology or archaeology of Kansas and especially of Rice County, of which Bushton is a part.

There is a great deal of fascinating history about Bushton and Kansas, of course, and Ally and I enjoyed learning much of it. Now, both of us have discovered an interest in geology and that, too, is a part of the history of Bushton, although a history from a much more distant past.

Chapter 5

Camels in Kansas?

Down a country road…

MEANWHILE, BACK AT THE SALT BEDS.

To truly understand Kansas one must know something of its geologic history. To get to the beginning, I've found you have to go back a few million years. A true geologist with much knowledge would want a more specific date but, for me, a "few million" years makes the point.

So, "a few million years ago" a large part of the North American continent was one huge sea. Eventually, somewhere south of Kansas a titanic upheaval evidently separated our northern part of this ocean and left the eventual site of Bushton in the middle of a gigantic saltwater lake. As this lake began slowly to evaporate, the salt found its way to the floor of the ocean (or lake) where, over centuries, it formed the salt beds and created an industry for today's Rice County.

Now we know that above the salt is a formation that is largely shale which has been under massive pressure for thousands (probably more than "a few thousand" years). Then came another sea which also brought sand and marine life. Some of the marine life eventually formed what is known as the Commanchean shale. A portion of that is visible not far from Bushton, just south of Little River in eastern Rice County.

Years later ("a few *** years – pick a number) another change occurred when the Arkansas River raged down from the Rocky Mountains, tore through the heart of the current Rice County and left a deposit of sand which eventually formed the Sand Hills in the southeastern and southwestern parts of the county, reaching as far north as the southern limits of the town of Lyons, our County Seat.

More recently – a somewhat fewer "million years" ago – more rivers poured down from the Rockies and leveled much of Kansas. At the same time there was much more moisture than today and this resulted in swamps with luxuriant vegetation which provided food for wandering animals. Some drowned in the massive rivers as they came to drink and others perhaps were caught in quicksand and were buried beneath the deposit of sand and gravel. Soon, geologically speaking, they had become petrified or fossil bones.

Some of these bones are still being discovered and geologists speculate that many of them, especially marine life, like the large "fish" on display at the Sternberg Museum in Hays, may have been washed into Kansas from as far west as those magnificent Rockies.

When was this?

Geologists say they have all been dead for at least 500,000 years or centuries before the Egyptian Pyramids were constructed and long before America was visited by Columbus and/or others.

In a book titled *The Story of Early Rice County* first published in 1929 by the author Horace Jones, then the editor of the *Lyons Daily News,* and republished in 1959 by his family, Jones lists a number of animals whose remains have been discovered in Kansas. The Kansas State Geological Survey also lists such now-extinct creatures as a large mastodon, a species of elephant, buffalo, moose, a small horse, a Peccary which is similar to a hog, a camel, a ground sloth and a large wolf. There were others, too.

After that, the land continued to erode and change, the flow of the rivers lessened, the swamps and luxuriant vegetation began to disappear and Kansas, and Rice County, slowly assumed the shape and make-up of today's countryside.

Many have raised the question of who might have been the first "white" men to visit central Kansas. Horace Jones wrote that many students of the subject now believe in the possibility that this section of the state may well have been the 400-year-old kingdom of Quivira and that not only Francisco Vasquez de Coronado but other early adventurers visited what is now Rice County nearly 100 years before the Pilgrims landed on Plymouth Rock. A museum in Lyons, Kansas, commemorates Coronado's visit and has other fascinating exhibits and information. Our Scout leader Mr. Timmons once took members of Troop 175 to Coronado Heights near Lindsborg, not too far east of Bushton, to view the site that could possibly mark the northeastern end of Coronado's explorations

Eventually, industry began to develop in Rice County and elsewhere in Kansas around the results of "a few million years" of water, sand, salt and erosion.

With that kind of historical knowledge Kansas, Rice County and Bushton begin to take on more meaningful and interesting significance.

80 – **REAL, RURAL**

Chapter 6

Mickey, Marilyn and a Singer.

Down a country road...

BUT LET'S GET BACK to "growing up rural."
It's been said that the '50s made up the decade of Mickey, Marilyn and Elvis. Maybe city kids were concerned during that time mainly with Mickey Mantle, Marilyn Monroe and Elvis Presley. I wasn't. Maybe some of my classmates were, but if so I don't know who they were.

We knew about Mickey Mantle and the New York Yankees, of course, but I didn't much care for them. To me, they represented too much money, a desire to win at all costs and big-city-Eastern-establishment dominance over the rest of the country. Give me the Cardinals, the Phillies, the Cubs and even the St. Louis Browns (remember them?). So Mickey made the papers now and then and, though I loved baseball with a passion and followed the scores, standings and World Series games, I was always glad to see that the Yankees had lost a game the previous day.

Despite that attitude, we're talking BASEBALL! As 1950s historian Jacques Barzun aptly observed: "Whoever wants to know the heart and mind of America had better learn baseball." For young people growing up (not just rural) during the fifties there was a great need for heroes which some believed was a metaphor for the human search of self-knowledge. Maybe so.

Our baseball field near the high school in Bushton had a dirt infield and no fences marking the boundary of the outfield. Sometimes a hit that might have been a single got past the shortstop or another infielder and rolled into the pasture way out there in the dark somewhere and became a home run.

In a 2019 book about Mickey Mantle called *The Best There Ever Was* author Tony Castro says this was the age when baseball players were the "princes of American sports," along with heavyweight boxers and Derby horses and the odd galloping ghost of a running back from down South or the occasional lanky basketball player in short shorts.

Castro called baseball an American cultural declaration of independence and said it has come to express the nation's character—perhaps never more so than during the intense, anti-Communist, post–World War II period, when a preoccupation with defining the national conscience might be expected, particularly defining the national self in a tradition that is so culturally middle-of-the-road. The period of which he was writing was, of course, the years in which my classmates and I were growing up, starting to become who we would be, forming attitudes, maturing (or not...), creating, and being created by, new bodies that helped define us as much as anything else. Baseball, and other sports, were a part of that growing-up process for the youth (boys and many of the girls) of Bushton.

But Mickey Mantle? He was a name from far away. He might as well have been in London which is a bit more than 4,500 miles "as the crow flies" from Bushton, Kansas.

Never mind that Mickey was from Oklahoma, where I was also born – in the doctor's office above the corner drug store on Route 66 which was the Main Street in the town of Chandler, Oklahoma.

Those of us who loved movies in the fifties (who didn't?) also knew of Marilyn Monroe. Most of us also knew that she hadn't always been a blond and that she had some personality quirks and other issues that made her difficult to work with on movie sets.

All of that wasn't particularly interesting to me until I met Ted White. Ted had been a stuntman, actor and director in films throughout the second half of the 20th Century. He worked with, doubled and was friends with such notables as John Wayne, Clark Gable, Rock Hudson, Kirk Douglas, Fess Parker, James

Dean and many others including Marilyn Monroe.

Little did I know, when I saw *The Misfits* starring Marilyn, Clark Gable and Montgomery Clift that the fellow wrestling with that wild horse was my friend Ted White and not Clark Gable or that I would later write Ted's biography (*Cast a Giant Shadow* —2017) and learn all about the problems the director (John Huston) and cast had with Marilyn Monroe. In the '50s, to me, she was simply another actress who made a lot of money and was interesting to see on screen.

She was simply, like Mickey Mantle, not that important to me.

Nor was Elvis.

I liked most of his music but didn't especially enjoy watching him during his performances. I have to admit I owned some of his records and I especially liked *Don't Be Cruel*, *Love Me Tender* and *All Shook Up*.

But there were others. I remember being simply blown away when driving one night in 1955 with the radio on (probably on my way to or from a date with Ally) and hearing, for the first time, *Sixteen Tons* by Tennessee Ernie Ford. Wow! That rhythmic beat, Ford's deep bass voice and lyrics like "another day older and deeper in debt" combined to make what seemed, at least that night, the perfect song.

And there were others that I have to believe anyone alive in the '50s would recall. Here are some of them: *Memories are Made of This* by Dean Martin, *Bye Bye Love* The Everly Brothers, *Blueberry Hill* Fats Domino, *Rock Around the Clock* Bill Haley and the Comets, *Love Letters in the Sand* Pat Boone, *Mack the Knife* Bobby Darin, *Moments to Remember* The Four Lads, and even Gogi Grant's *The Wayward Wind*.

Remember those? How could you not?

Likewise, there were the movies. *On the Waterfront*, *Bridge on the River Kwai*, *Singin' in the Rain*, the James Dean trio of *Rebel Without a Cause* and *East of Eden* in 1955 and *Giant* in '56, *Ben Hur*, *Invasion of the Body Snatchers*, *The Searchers*, *The Wild One* and of course *Picnic* which was filmed largely in Kansas, not far from Bushton.

I even had a red jacket that I believed was like the one

James Dean wore in *Rebel Without a Cause*. I wore it a lot.

Interestingly, while Mantle was hitting homers, playing injured and drinking too much, but still being hailed as a hero and heir to Babe Ruth's fame, and Elvis was cranking out hit after hit (and terrifying many adults across the country) Monroe's films were doing only fair at the box office. Only three of her movies ended a year in the top ten – *The Seven Year Itch* in 1955, *Bus Stop* in 1956 and *Some Like it Hot* in 1959.

Meanwhile, an upstart rebel named Marlon Brando appeared first on stage and then in the movie version of *A Streetcar Named Desire* and received rave notices while increasing the heartrate of countless young women. Remember the "Stella!" scream?

Brando is widely considered the greatest movie actor of all time, rivaled only by the more theatrically oriented Laurence Olivier in terms of esteem, according to the website https://www.imdb.com.

Brando received an Academy Award, for his performance as Terry Malloy in *On the Waterfront*, and his portrayal of the rebellious motorcycle gang leader Johnny Strabler in *The Wild One* proved to be a lasting image in popular culture. He received Academy Award nominations for playing Emiliano Zapata in *Viva Zapata!* (1952); Mark Antony in Joseph L. Mankiewicz's 1953 film adaptation of Shakespeare's *Julius Caesar*; and Air Force Major Lloyd Gruver in *Sayonara* (1957), an adaptation of James Michener's 1954 novel.

As for Marilyn Monroe, the film *The Misfits* came out in 1961 and was to be her last movie role. She died the next year.

But life goes on. The public can forgive and forget (Mantle's drinking, Monroe's problems and Elvis' long hair and bodily gyrations) and remember only their talents and achievements, however dubious or unwelcome in Bible Belt Kansas and much of the rest of the country.

Looking back, it's interesting to realize that all three – Mantle, Monroe and Elvis – died in the month of August – Monroe in 1962 at age 36, Elvis (or is he still alive?) in 1977 at age 42, and Mantle in 1995 at age 63.

Achilles is supposed to have said: "The Gods envy us

because we're mortal, because any moment may be our last. Everything is more beautiful because we're doomed."

Did each of these three "famous" people have some fatal flaw that led to their doom?

To a teenager in rural Kansas in the '50s (at least to this one) those personalities weren't that important and I wouldn't call the fifties, as some in the East did, "The Decade of Mantle, Monroe and Elvis." None of the three were, to me at least, what might be termed heroes. They were well-known for their particular field but they were also a long way from Kansas and had no real significant impact on the lives of many of us who were more concerned with other things, other people, other matters that were of far greater importance to each individual.

There was much going on in the fifties, however, that was more significant than baseball, movies and rock 'n roll. But it's fun to think about those years and how the events of the day helped form our young lives, even from faraway New York or Los Angeles.

86 – **REAL, RURAL**

Chapter 7

Stick shifts, Studebakers and McCarthyism

Down a country road...

IN 1945 FORMER BRITISH Prime Minister Winston Churchill stated that "America, at this moment, stands at the summit of the world." It seems that he was right. By the 1950s, and even before then, the U.S. was the world's strongest military power and its economy was the best it had ever been.

That was evident in the fifties in the appearance of new cars, new suburbs and new homes and stores full of new consumer goods. It was felt even in small towns like Bushton.

Millie (Heiken) Sanderson ('56) recalls that, in the fifties "we had a car with running boards." Quickly enough, those running boards disappeared and new, sleeker, more powerful automobiles began to appear on streets and roads everywhere.

I recall that sometime in the mid-fifties Jim Hudson, an assistant coach and commerce teacher in the high school, not much older than some of us – a recent graduate of Southwestern College, a small private Methodist-related college in Winfield, Kansas – showed up in a brand new Ford (I think it was a convertible!) and wowed all the high school students, including me. Man, it was the coolest!

Speaking of cars. My family always seemed to have a good car. They included Chevys, Studebakers, Pontiacs, Fords and others. This was because my Dad's job required driving to oil wells, pumping units or drilling rigs throughout his territory (basically central Kansas). He always had "pump racks" welded on the passenger side of any car he drove on business so he could easily carry pipe and pumps. The U-shaped racks would be screwed into the pieces welded onto the vehicle and removed when necessary (when I was allowed to use the car for a date with Ally, for example, or when the family was taking a trip).

The family's second car was a 1952 Studebaker. Yes, we had two cars. Mainly because my Dad was on the road a great deal and Mom needed transportation at home. That old Studebaker, a green one with a bullet nose, saw me through high school and into college. Ally remembers it well, too.

My Mom and our '52 Studebaker. The grain elevator looms in the background.

The first time I was allowed to take the car (the Studebaker, naturally) out on my own was an early Easter morning, probably in 1955, following a Sunrise Service at the Methodist Church. I think Phil Henry ('57) and another girl (I don't remember who it was) rode with Ally and me as I maneuvered the car safely around the small town. There were few other vehicles on the streets at that hour. The Studebaker was a stick shift and Phil kept telling me that I was shifting gears too often. As I recall, I didn't think so.

At any rate, that car was the one in which I learned to drive by backing it down the long driveway from our garage to the street, shifting to low gear, driving back to the garage, and then repeating the process over and over. I'm sure my parents thought there was something wrong with me.

Ally says she learned to drive in a plowed field. Sounds

pretty rough to me. I like the idea of a long driveway better.

Ally and I had many dates in that old car. I'm sure everyone in Bushton came to recognize it and I suspect they would shake their heads when they saw it and wonder why we hung onto it so long.

Many of my friends from the fifties brought up the topic of driving, most at an early age. Sue Dahlsten, for example, said she drove from the time she was about 11 years old. "I would drive the old tractor and my Dad and brother would pitch hay on the hay wagon. Then to the barn to pitch it all into the haymow."

Sue said she drove the wheat truck during harvest and "would bring the truck to our elevator and shovel it into the bin." She said a wheat beard once few into her eye and the next morning the eye was swollen shut. That left her father to do the jobs Sue had been doing. "Needless to say, he was happy to have me back" when her eye mended.

Wayne Groth said he started driving a car when he was 13. "It didn't seem that unusual, and given that I was already driving a tractor that was a lot more powerful than a car, it didn't seem like a major leap to driving a car."

Don Hiltbrunner (Hoot) said he got a driver's license at the age of 14 (a "restricted" one). He remembered learning to do a "spin out" behind the school building, driving to the movie in Holyrood, going to the high school dances after a game, and "smooching a honey afterwards while parked in the dark near her home."

Kansas youth could get a license to drive with "restrictions" at age 14. That kind of license allowed them to drive when an adult was along, to drive to and from school and to run errands for parents. The license was designed mainly for farm kids but "townies" could get the same license.

Myretta Bell said, as a result, farm kids had the jump on townies because they had long been driving tractors and trucks. "The teens stretched the limits of the driving restrictions though," Myretta said. "Every year a group of new eighth graders who had just turned 14 – and maybe others of questionable age – pushed the limits of the restrictions on the streets around town."

I hate to admit it but, when I took my first driving test to get that restricted license, I failed. I couldn't parallel park. I'd never had to. In Bushton, there was no need. I did pass the test the second time I tried.

Myretta tells a familiar story about driving home after school at age 16 with four other students when she got stuck on a muddy road after a hard rain. She left her passengers and walked to the nearby farm of Marvin Weihe who freed her car with his tractor. "No complaint, no money accepted, just a good neighbor," she said. She emphasized that there were very few paved roads in Rice County in those days and that her route to and from school was all on dirt roads.

Learning to drive often involved the parents of "new" drivers. Lanara Luthi said there was no driver training in school so country roads provided the opportunity for parents to do the teaching. She said her father sat in the middle of the front seat during training sessions so he could "grab the wheel or stomp the brakes" if necessary. Her little sisters sat in the back observing the "no trespassing" rules of the "invisible line" in the back seat. "Mom clung to the door of the passenger seat, also in front. She thought she had a legitimate reason to fear for her life, especially when crossing those little concrete bridges over the creeks." Lanara said she "had a tendency to hug the right side of the road." She was "free-wheeling," she said. "I didn't let Mom's whimpering bother me at all."

In the fifties, our Studebaker was very important to me. It afforded more and more opportunities to see Ally and, like an adult, drive her to movies or other events out of town.

Even more important, but of lesser interest to us than significant local events, was the fact that the fifties included substantial conflict at home and abroad. The beginning of the Civil Rights Movement, for example, clearly exposed the divisions in American society and at the same time America joined and, in many ways, led the crusade against Communism.

Remember "McCarthyism?" It is recalled by some with incredulity but with bitter anger by others. The website https://www.britannica.com defines McCarthyism as the name given to the period of time in American history that saw Wisconsin Sen. Joseph McCarthy produce a series of investigations and hearings during the 1950s in an effort to expose supposed communist infiltration of various areas of the U.S. government. The term has since become a byname for defamation of character or reputation by means of widely publicized indiscriminate allegations, especially on the basis of unsubstantiated charges.

McCarthy rose to prominence in 1950 when he claimed in a speech that more than 200 communists had infiltrated the State Department. McCarthy's subsequent search for communists in the Central Intelligence Agency, the State Department, and elsewhere made him an incredibly polarizing figure.

McCarthy was eventually undermined significantly by the incisive and skillful criticism of a journalist, Edward R. Murrow, whose devastating television editorial about McCarthy, presented on his show *See It Now*, cemented him as the premier journalist of the time. McCarthy was censured for his conduct by the Senate, and in 1957 he died. The website notes that while McCarthyism proper ended with the Senator's downfall, the term still has currency in modern political discourse.

Edward R. Murrow, who many students of the fifties remember well, was the inspiration for many aspiring journalists long before Watergate and the *Washington Post's* famous reporters Woodward and Bernstein.

Wayne Groth said he doesn't really recall McCarthy but he does have a good recollection of one particular event. "I remember a Scout meeting where we were given a book to help us identify Soviet planes," he said. The concept, he believes, was to develop a civil defense system in each community that involved the public keeping an eye out for Soviet planes. "It's hard to imagine how a Soviet plane could be seen in Kansas air space without being detected earlier," he said. "I wish I still had that book."

While we were somewhat aware of the McCarthyism drama going on in the East, we were, no doubt, more interested in Friday's football game, a weekend or evening job that would provide spending money, a date for the dance after the game, getting one's chores done at home, an upcoming slumber party or getting that driver's license.

Throughout the country families were growing. It was called the "baby boom." The "boom" began in 1946 when about three and a half million babies were born in the U.S. It continued through much of the fifties when about four million babies were born each year. When the "boom" finally tapered off in 1964, there were almost 77 million "baby boomers."

The economy continued to grow and more than doubled between 1945 and 1960. Much of this increase, statistics show, came from government spending: new Interstate highways, new schools, veterans' benefits and spending on the military for goods like airplanes and on new technologies like computers. Rates of unemployment and inflation were low and, generally, wages were high. Middle-class people (like many in Bushton) had more money to spend than ever and there were more "things" available to buy.

This new affluence was made more apparent with the construction of many new suburban "Levitttown" communities in the East which afforded thousands (perhaps millions) of young couples their first opportunity for home ownership but which quickly attracted much criticism from city-bound pundits. Also, about this same time, discount stores and shopping centers (malls) began to appear.

Other changes were also afoot. Women had quickly become disillusioned with the roles they had been assigned after the conclusion of World War II and the return of millions of men. They felt that, for example, the "booms" of the fifties, perhaps especially the "baby" boom, had a confining effect on many of them. Advice books and articles in newspapers and magazines – "Don't be Afraid to Marry Young," "Cooking to Me is Poetry," "Femininity Begins at Home" and many others – built on the idea that a woman's most important jobs were to bear and raise children and do their husbands' bidding.

In her 1963 book *The Feminine Mystique* (published by W.W. Norton) women's rights advocate Betty Friedan said she believed the suburbs, and by extension changing attitudes about women and their roles, were burying women alive. This would ultimately lead to the rebirth of the feminist movement in the sixties.

Myretta Bell remembers that "after the war the U.S. government actually printed a pamphlet telling 'Rosie the Riveter' to resign from her job and return home so returning military personnel could have her job."

Myretta says when occupations were illustrated in literature, even "as early as first grade, women could be teachers, nurses or secretaries." Men could be anything, she said, "so if a woman could afford college, she could be a teacher or nurse. If not, she could go to business school and be a secretary."

In Bushton, Myretta recalled, there were few jobs for females. She said women could get a job as cashier at the bank, secretary at school, clerk at the drug store selling sodas and wedding gifts selected by prospective brides, clerk at the grain elevator, switch operator at the telephone company, hairdresser at home or music teacher at home. "That's not many jobs for all the women in town," she said.

A survey of the time spent in the home by most housewives of the '50s, quoted by Marguerite Pattan in *Post War Kitchen: Nostalgic Food and Facts from 1945 to 1954*, established that, on average, they worked 75 hours a week, with overtime on Saturdays and Sundays. This did not take into account that a number of women were also doing part or fulltime work outside the home.

A popular saying of the decade was "all work and no pay makes Jackie a housewife."

Sara Sheridan said writing about the 1950s gave her tremendous respect for her mother's generation. Sheridan is the author of several books including *The World of Sanditon*.

And Tory Telfer suggests, in *Lady Killers: Deadly Women Throughout History* that we should think of everything cliché we know about the 1950s. That includes housewives spending their days vacuuming with martinis in hand and a look of existential horror in their eyes, and every home being outfitted with a TV set.

But, Myretta insisted, "farm wives were a different breed."

If you were a farm wife, she said, "you might milk cows, tend chickens, drive a tractor pulling equipment, drive a truck, take home-cooked meals to workers in the field, paint the exterior of a small building, paint the interior of your home and provide transportation for your children's school activities in addition to doing the laundry, cooking, child caring, housecleaning and community or church activities."

But Myretta wasn't through. "Then there was the garden," she said. "All farm families had a garden. Period. Often a farmer's livelihood depended on the garden. Wheat was still the main crop in the fifties but if the wheat crop was disastrous due to hail, too little rain, too much rain, too much wind, too many weeds or too hot weather, the garden produce and any livestock helped them through the winter with the hope next year's crop would be a bonanza."

Other Bushton High School grads echoed Myretta's thoughts. Lanara Luthi said she and her family planted a garden every year in the back yard of their home. "The food was always good," she said, "but it didn't seem to last very long."

Likewise, Sue Dahlsten said "we grew or raised almost everything we needed. We had chickens, pigs, cattle, a garden, and an orchard."

Families helped the "kids" focus on the fact that we were mainly concerned with growing food (or raising it in the way of cattle or chickens, for example), or making enough money to purchase what we needed.

In addition, most of us probably didn't give a great deal of thought in the fifties to a growing group of Americans who were speaking out against inequality and injustice. Bushton, like most of the small towns in the state at that time, was almost totally white. While African Americans had been fighting against racial discrimination for centuries, it wasn't until the fifties that the struggle against racism and segregation entered the mainstream of American life.

The fact that racism and segregation was prominent, even in Kansas, was brought home clearly in 1954 when, in the landmark Brown v. Board of Education case in Topeka, Kansas, the Supreme Court declared that "separate educational facilities" for black children were "inherently unequal."

Much of America was stunned with the unanimous

decision of the Supreme Court. Some think the resolution of the case was the single most important moment in the decade. Some say it instantaneously broadened the concept of freedom and that this decision was just the beginning of a startling new period of change…in all aspects of social behavior.

We were to learn that this ruling was the first nail in Jim Crow's coffin.

Jo (Lindsay) Hodges ('57) does recall, however, that racial prejudice was evident, even in our small town. "When black men came to work on the railroad tracks," she said, "they were not allowed downtown after dark."

I never gave that much thought, even if I was aware of it. In fact, I didn't know any black people at all until the summer Neil Denton and I played baseball for an American Legion team in the neighboring town of Holyrood. A young shortstop with an arm like a cannon also played on that team. He was black. As I recall I didn't give much thought to that fact. He was a good ballplayer who could hit and field. And he was a nice guy. That's all that mattered.

In another instance, I happened to be spending time with a cousin in Chandler, Oklahoma (the town in which I was born), and was in the city swimming pool when it was integrated. I remember wondering why so many white kids left the pool when a few African Americans showed up in swimming suits. I stayed in, as I recall, and thought no more about it.

Looking back, I now wish I had paid more attention to what was going on in the world as it related to black/white relationships. I know I was at least a bit dismayed when I learned of the way black people had been treated over the past (how many?) decades but, I must have thought, nothing like that was going on in central Kansas. So why should I worry? I now know that I should definitely have worried. There must have been something I could have done. There must be something I could still do. There are few black folks near where I now live. I dislike the idea that African Americans are still the object of disdain on the part of many and I don't understand that attitude. I hope and pray that, had I been brought up in the South where so many of the acts of segregation which included hatred, fear and violence took place, that I would have reacted differently from what did occur.

Even after the Brown v. Board of Education ruling, many southern whites, in an act of resistance, withdrew their children from public schools, enrolled them in all-white "segregation academies," and turned to violence and intimidation to prevent blacks from asserting their rights. In 1956 more than 100 southern congressmen signed a "Southern Manifesto" declaring that they would do all they could to defend segregation.

However, a new movement was born in December of 1955 when a Montgomery, Alabama, activist named Rosa Parks was arrested for refusing to give her seat on a city bus to a white person. Her arrest sparked a 13-month boycott of the city's buses by its black citizens. Acts of "nonviolent resistance" like this boycott help shape the civil rights movement of the next decade. Hers was a tireless campaign.

She is quoted as saying: "The only tired it was, was the tired of giving in."

When Rosa Parks died in 2005 she was the first woman to lie in honor in the Rotunda of the U.S. Capitol.

In Bushton, Kansas, we read about her in the *Wichita Eagle,* the *Great Bend Tribune* or the *Hutchinson News,* watched the Civil Rights movement unfold on television, and probably thought "good for her" and let it go at that. I don't remember her brave act being a topic of discussion in any of my classes. But that doesn't mean it didn't happen. No doubt, I was concerned with other, "more important," local matters – the upcoming basketball game, Ally, what movie was being shown next in Holyrood, Ally, what was for dinner that evening, Ally, whether I would be able to get a job on a farm that summer, Ally. We might well have discussed Rosa Parks but I simply don't remember it.

If we didn't, I wish we had.

As a young journalist (and now an "older" one) I have been especially interested in how the Civil Rights movement affected the development of television news. A young NBC newscaster named John Chancellor gained early fame while covering the beginning segregation efforts in Montgomery, Alabama, and was one of the first to not only recognize the power of this relatively new visual medium but also learn how to use it to its best advantage. Chancellor was considered a pioneer in TV news. He served as anchor of the NBC Nightly News from 1970 to 1982 and worked with Tom Brokaw until 1992. He died in 1996.

Remember the "Cold War?" This tension between the United States and the Soviet Union was another defining element of the fifties. Western leaders worried that the USSR had "expansive tendencies" and they believed that the spread of communism anywhere threatened democracy and capitalism everywhere. The idea that communism must be "contained" helped shape American foreign policy for decades.

Still, the booming prosperity of the fifties helped to create a widespread sense of stability, contentment and consensus. We felt that way in Bushton. But, at the same time, the U.S. was a nation that believed it was on the edge of nuclear war.

Here are some more of the especially significant events, tensions and beliefs that made their ways into the minds of many of us in Bushton during the fifties.

Political tensions were high.

Communists took control of one eastern European nation after another and the fact that Russia had the atomic bomb set off a nuclear arms race.

The Korean War, begun when North Korea invaded South Korea in 1950, spurred American efforts to develop a weapon even more deadly than the atomic bomb. That weapon became the hydrogen bomb. Many Americans built bomb shelters in their back yards. I don't remember any being constructed in Bushton but I could be mistaken.

The aforementioned Richard Rhodes would later write a book (published in 1995) called *Dark Sun* about the making of the hydrogen bomb and the growing fears of devastation during the Cold War.

The Korean War was being fought in a land far from our shores and no one seemed to want it. Although the country had been declared of little strategic value it seemed as though the war was something that needed to be done. We seemed to want no part of the country, but yet we had planted the flag and felt we had to carry through.

Meanwhile, in the U.S. life went on.

In 1950 almost one and a half million new homes were built in America, mostly by optimistic young people. Most of these new houses were located in suburbs, areas outside cities. People moved to the suburbs, they said, because they thought the schools were better than city schools. Imagine that.

In 1952 Americans elected Dwight Eisenhower, a military hero of World War II and a Kansan, President.

The 1950s brought the Barbie Doll, the Frisbee and the Hula Hoop. Poodle cuts were for women who wanted to look "stylish."

The '50s also saw the emergence of a chain of small hamburger restaurants known as McDonald's and a motel chain that quickly spread across the country – the Holiday Inn.

We know about cultural icons James Dean and Marilyn Monroe but there were also writers who were having an influence on the youth of the fifties, even in Bushton, Kansas. Some came to be known as the "Beat Generation" and included Jack Kerouac, Gregory Corso and Allen Ginsberg.

I read their works but especially Kerouac's *On the Road* and thought at the time it was wonderful literature.

In music, as we also know, the rebel was Elvis Presley – the king of rock 'n roll. He was a 21year-old truck driver when he sang on television for the first time. While some parents and religious leaders thought he was a bad influence, young people, many in Bushton, screamed for more.

Television in the fifties included dramas, quiz shows and comedy programs. As I wrote in *Cast a Giant Shadow*, the period beginning in the late 1940s and extending to the late 1950s or early 1960s has been dubbed "The Golden Age of Television" as 77 percent of American households purchased their first TV set during that time.

Wayne Groth recalled that "the arrival of the first TV for our family was at my grandmother's house." He thinks that was around 1955. "I spent a lot of time in front of that TV watching Red Skelton and Ed Sullivan," he said. "Grandma always had a refrigerator stocked with Pepsi Cola which was another reason to go visit her. The front door was never locked and she was always glad to see us."

I recall seeing television for the first time during a visit to relatives in Oklahoma. I was entranced by the small, somewhat oval and nearly light green image. The program wasn't especially memorable but the actuality of sitting in one's living room and watching something like film unfold on a small, confined screen in front of me was mesmerizing.

In the meantime, even though members of the so-called "Beat Generation" rebelled against conventional values and Hugh Hefner launched *Playboy* magazine in 1953 the fifties are seen by some today as the "best time" when families and morals were intact and times were simpler and enjoyable.

During much of the fifties, cowboy programs prevailed on television and at any one time there were as many as 120 Western series on the small screen. As a teenager in Bushton, Kansas, I was glad the good guy wore the white hat and always won. "Look both ways when you get to the curbside and don't forget to go to Sunday school," Hopalong Cassidy always said at the end of his show. That was good advice although the small amount of traffic in Bushton surely spoiled the kids, and I probably often forgot to look both ways. I kind of wanted a Hopalong Cassidy wristwatch but I never bought one. However, I did go to Sunday School.

The myth propagated by the movie or TV Western tells a prettier story than what really happened. Americans, including the cowboy whom we mistakenly associated with Roy Rogers, Randolph Scott, John Wayne and others, including even *Shane* himself, subjugated Native Americans, plundered and killed and raped and lied about whoever had what they wanted. And when the dust had settled they owned everything from one coast to the other including gold, water, land or whatever else they wanted.

But, in the fifties, Lucille Ball reigned as the queen of comedy with millions of viewers tuned weekly to *I Love Lucy*.

And remember Ed Sullivan, Milton Berle, Jackie Gleason and Sid Caesar?

And color TV beginning in a small way in 1953?

Still, during the fifties most of those appearing on TV

were white. If black actors appeared, they were usually in jobs working for white people. In real life the Civil Rights movement was gathering strength.

Eisenhower was President and, even though he was facing problems of communism, nuclear threats and racial tension, "Ike" had a calm way of speaking to the public and many Americans saw him as a fatherly President. They thought that even in a dark and dangerous world, everything would be all right.

To many of us in rural Bushton, Kansas, that was true, at least as I recall, among the young folks.

While the fifties are remembered for any number of important events, people and inventions, the decade stands out in the minds of many people – especially women – because of one iconic little pill. After millennia of attempts to figure out ways to prevent conception, the Birth Control Pill made its appearance in the 1950s.

We are reminded that the very concept of birth control is not modern by Linda Gordon, then a history professor at NYU who penned the definitive history of birth control in America, 1976's *Woman's Body, Woman's Right: A Social History of Birth Control in America* (updated and republished in 2004 as *The Moral Property of Women: A History of Birth Control Politics in America*). Gordon claimed that even in the most ancient and primitive societies, anthropologists have discovered, people were attempting to control their fertility.

Andrea Tone, a professor of history at McGill University penned one of the most authoritative books on the subject – *Devices and Desires: A History of Contraceptives in America* (Published in 2002 by Hill and Wang).

When the organized fight for contraception started taking shape, the face of this movement was a charismatic and ambitious woman named Margaret Sanger, regarded today as the person most responsible for transforming birth control from a widespread private practice into a political, public movement. While working as a visiting nurse in New York, Sanger was "appalled" by the poor health of lower-class women giving birth to children they couldn't afford — or resorting to dangerous back-alley abortions. In 1921, she founded the organization that would later become Planned Parenthood.

In 1957, the FDA approved the Pill — but only for the treatment of menstrual disorders. Coincidentally, an estimated 500,000 women quickly reported having such disorders. Then in 1960, the FDA OK'd the Pill to prevent pregnancy.

In addition to the backlash from conservative Americans and religious institutions like the Catholic Church, which had officially banned birth control in 1930, there were many substantial obstacles to surmount before the Pill would reach the status it enjoys today.

Looking back today, it can be difficult to grasp just how major the impact of the Pill was on life for American women. Many believe that effective contraception was probably in the whole of the 20th century the most important change for women. They believe the ability to be in control of their own fertility and reproduction gave women a profound new autonomy over their own bodies, their health, and their sexuality. The Pill hugely factored into the sexual revolution of the '60s

Birth control has become imperceptibly woven into the fabric of society, a prerequisite for modern life – as unremarkable and taken-for-granted as many of the rest of our most miraculous technological innovations.

Chapter 8

Everything we Needed

Down a country road…

IT TAKES A LIFETIME to build a life, and M. T. Edvardsson, the author of *A Nearly Normal Family*, a book published by Celadon Books in 2019, believes it takes many years, decades, maybe a lifetime, to become the person you truly are. He said the path is almost always circuitous and he believed there was a reason for that, for life to be built around trial and error. Most agree that we are shaped and created by our trials.

If that is true, and I suspect it is, then we who were raised rural were shaped differently from those who grew up in a city. Our trials, and our errors, were determined as much by our environment as they were driven by our inner selves, the "who" we are at any given moment and the hopes and desires and needs that propel us one way or another in an instant, without thought or preparation. Because of who and what we are in that instant, we just "do" or "don't do."

Bushton, Kansas, her people and her values and history helped shape my life.

Just as important – no doubt moreso – were my parents.

Likewise, the parents of my classmates had their own roles to play in helping shape the lives of their children.

In my case, and I'm sure in the case of my sister, I was fortunate. Fortunate to have landed in Bushton at a time when I desperately needed the kind of life experiences I found there. Fortunate to have been born to Lawrence and Eva Meredith. Fortunate to have been encouraged to try and make something of myself. And I was fortunate to have met and fallen in love with a pretty blue-eyed girl nicknamed Ally whose firm hand and proper role modeling would also play an important and treasured role in shaping my life. First, Bushton. What kind of town was it?

Dale Nordstrom lived in Bushton from his birth until he went away to college after high school graduation in 1955. "To my knowledge," he said "Bushton has always been very homogeneous: of German origin, white Christian (Catholic and Protestant), no Jews, African Americans or Hispanics while I was growing up. As far as I know there were never any riots, shootings or crime of any kind. If there was it was kept under wraps."

Fran Habiger ('56) said "Bushton had just about everything we needed." He said "it had a hotel, two barbershops, a lumberyard, a machinery dealer, a bank, café, two car and tractor repair shops, a hardware store, a Chevrolet dealer, two grocery stores, an ice plant and the telephone office."

It also had a drugstore, a library, a grain elevator, a pool hall, a couple of churches and a post office.

Speaking of the drugstore, Joy Nickerson worked there during her high school years. "Some of my best memories," she said, "are getting to see so many happy faces at the soda fountain." She called working there "a very happy experience" and added that "there was no crime, no TV and no cell phones."

But there was a newspaper. The weekly *Bushton News* was printed in another town but we received it every week and eagerly looked forward to reading about ourselves in the sports news, finding out who had hosted a dinner last Friday night, and how many people attended a birthday party for one of our older residents. My sister Linda says "it was fun and you never knew when you might be surprised at seeing your name in the paper!"

Lanara Luthi also mentions a "beauty shop." She said the beauty shop had a metal hood with heated curlers dangling. "Oh how we suffered for our beauty!" She said she "received that benefit upon entering first grade. Needless to say, every hair on my head fuzzed because of the electric curler. Good grief! I hated the look!" She said that occasionally her mother took her to the barber shop for a haircut. "Gene Braden, the barber, was a nice man but that was a shop for men and boys! Yuk!"

The two grocery stores in Bushton allowed customers to

have charge accounts, according to Fran Habiger. He said accounts were kept on tickets that resided in a clipboard that had all the customers' names and the amount they owed. "Periodically," he said, "we would go into the store" and "settle up."

He also remembered that, though many of the families in Bushton raised their own chickens, at least one of the grocery stores kept live chickens. "When someone wanted a chicken for dinner," he said, "the store clerk caught one, butchered it on the spot and sent it home with the customer."

Those chickens also provided fresh eggs for customers says Joy Nickerson who also said one "could buy dry beans or fresh fruit right out of a wooden barrel by the counter."

Fran also noted that the Mercantile had a large freezer in the back of the store and families could rent bins to store their meats. "We butchered a lot," Fran said. "When our mother decided to have pork chops, for example, we went to town, got the key to our bin and retrieved what we needed." The freezer bins disappeared, he said, when everyone eventually purchased their own freezers.

Some of the families had milk delivered to their homes by local farmers who actually milked the cows. "The farmer would bring gallon jars full of milk with the cream floating to the top," said Lanara Luthi. "We had to mix it up before serving because we kids hated those bits of cream swimming around in the glass." She said about once a year the cows would get into some kind of weird weed which caused the milk to taste horrible. "We drank it anyway with much complaining," she said.

Shirley Mullenix ('57), who lived near the railroad tracks like I did, says she "always liked waving to passengers on the numerous trains that passed through and to the men who stayed in the boxcars by the railroad tracks." She said Bushton had a full-service gas station where the men "did everything for you including washing your windows and pumping the gas for you."

In addition to all of that, my sister Linda found defining elements of Bushton in sunflowers, wind, windmills, oil wells and oil well pumps and wheatfields. "This little town was anything but sleepy at that point in time," she said. She called it "a magical place for kids" and said Bushton "enveloped its citizens with a place to belong. It gave us a place to run and play, all over town! It was the place where we would form life-long friendships, learn the multiplication tables and learn to worship our God."

Like Linda, several of those with whom I spoke talked of their love of windmills. They mentioned how the old windmills on farms punctuated the Kansas sky in those days but have now been largely replaced with the massive turbines that line the Kansas horizon in many places and create wind-generated electricity.

Ally's father Vernon had a tall windmill just outside the front door of their farmhouse. At the top he had installed a large television antenna. Once, when our then very young daughter Suzy was in a questioning mood, she asked how Grampa made the television picture better by doing something to the windmill. That was one of her easier questions to answer.

Don "Hoot" Hiltbrunner called Bushton "a quiet, clean, high-maintained village with beautiful trees, manicured lawns, blessed with Mayor Jurgen Hafferman overseeing it all." In addition to the businesses recalled by others, Hoot mentioned "a railroad track with a noisy train that never stopped, spit benches in front of the pool hall and barbershop and a meaningful (grades 1 through 12) schoolhouse that was the centerpiece of the town."

Hoot also included Kenny Feist's TV/Radio repair shop which was located between Nordstrom's Plumbing and the Hotel. Kenny, Hoot said, was Leo Feist's son and he was just back from the Korean War.

Dale Nordstrom had lots of memories about Bushton's "Sports Parlor," the pool hall, Rex Huebner, proprietor. He said the stories he told about the place made it sound like he spent all his free time there. "It's not true," he declared.

Linda recalls that she always walked on the west side of Main Street "in order to avoid walking by the pool hall." Who knew," she wondered, "what evil went on inside those doors?"

Dale Nordstrom said thinking about the pool hall reminded him of Billy, a mentally challenged youngster in the movie *The Last Picture Show* based on the novel of the same name written by Larry McMurtry and published in 1966. Dale said "Thalia, the town in the movie and novel, had a few more affairs than Bushton maybe: I was a little ignorant of happenings, but I think Bushton had the same soul. It had its characters."

The character who reminded him of "Billy" was our own Billy Schlagle. "He just hung around town and the pool hall," Dale said, "being a friendly pest." He recalled other "characters" who spent a great deal of time in the pool hall and said "the Saturday after losing a basketball or football game, the pool hall was where you went to find out what you did wrong. A bunch of old 'codgers' were willing to give you advice."

A lot of those old "codgers" had nicknames and Fran Habiger recalled many of them. "As I was growing up," he said, "I would hear my parents talking about 'Hunter' Hall, 'Barney' Mehl or 'Bud' Peterson." Fran said his favorite, though, is the fellow whose last name was Frye and was known all of his life as "Chicken." He said "Shorty" Blank ('56) from his class printed "Shorty" on his nametag at a recent class reunion. He also recalled "Popeye" Apple ('45) and Don Hiltbrunner who, soon after moving to Bushton, became "Hoot."

All my Dad's brothers and his sister had nicknames. They are, from left: Clarence (Mutt), Truman (Doc), Lawrence, my Dad (Chub), Lorene (Beanie), Lowell (Pegg) and Lloyd (Sug).

Bushton was initially, and for many years, a "farming"

community made up of folks who understood and appreciated agriculture. Several businesses focused on providing services and equipment of an agricultural nature.

That began to change early in the 1930s when oil was first discovered two miles north of town on the farm of Dale Nordstrom's grandfather, Ed Heiken. "I don't know anything about his finances but Ed became the 'go to' guy for folks who couldn't or wouldn't get a loan at the Bushton State Bank," Dale said. "He kept names and payments in a small, pocket-sized spiral notebook. As far as I know he was never 'stiffed' on any loan. If you didn't make your payments," Dale said, there were those "who would make sure you did."

"Nobody was rich (to my knowledge)," Dale said, "except William Volkland, the banker who was our next door neighbor." He said there were some college graduates, but not even all the school teachers had college degrees. The major occupations were farming, working in the oil fields and the few small businesses. Northern Natural Gas became the largest single employer.

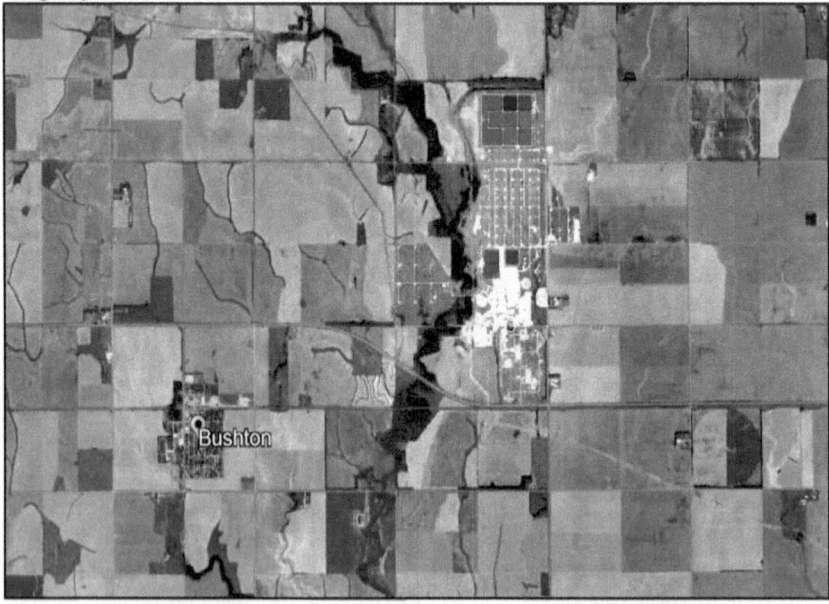

Another GoogleEarth Landsat photo showing Bushton in the lower left and the Northern Natural Gas Company station in the center which is to the northeast of Bushton.

Northern's website says Northern Natural Gas is a subsidiary of Berkshire Hathaway Energy based in Omaha, Nebraska, and has been in business since 1930. Northern owns and operates the largest interstate natural gas pipeline system in the United States. Its pipeline system stretches across 11 states, from the Permian Basin in Texas to Michigan's Upper Peninsula, providing access to five of the major natural gas supply regions in North America.

The station at Bushton, the website says, is owned by Kansas Gas Service, a division of One Gas, Inc.

The aforementioned Ed Heiken was also the grandfather of Millie Sanderson and she recalled a story about her father, who graduated from Bushton in 1924. She said his father, Ed, wanted him to be a minister and sent him to Kansas Wesleyan College in Salina. Millie said her father didn't want to be a preacher. He wanted to farm and wanted "the best polled milking shorthorns he could buy."

Millie said she was the "third born daughter" and was raised on the farm. Her mother, a graduate of Palmer High School in Colorado Springs, was the only high school graduate in her family. "I guess my family always had money for 'things,'" Millie said. "We always had a piano in the house, although I only knew how to play the right hand."

Wayne Groth says he always considered that his "growing up" was "on the farm and not the small town of Bushton that was five miles away." He said he doesn't recall during that period of time ever "being isolated from the activities in town."

As I recall, it might have been nearly impossible to be isolated from the activities in town, whether you lived within the city limits or not.

Gwen Lord certainly didn't feel isolated. In fact she said "the best thing I remember is that I never worried about not being safe." She said she even felt free to explore the creek which was "a mile down the road."

Gwen's sister Jo (Lindsay) Hodges ('57) had much the same feeling. "I couldn't have lived in a better place as a child," she said. She feels living in Bushton helped her "build more trust in people." She said she might have trusted people more than she should have "which I learned about when I moved to California – like locking doors and people keeping their word."

My sister Linda also made comments about "trust." Walking to or from school or town she had to cross the railroad tracks. "I would often pass men working on the tracks," she said. "They were all strangers to me and I felt sorry for them having to do that hard work away from their own hometowns." She would smile at them and say hello. "Somehow," she said, "my parents heard about this (via the small town grapevine?) and cautioned me not to speak to men I didn't know." She said that was the first time she "began to understand that I shouldn't expect everyone in the world to be loving and trustworthy like the people I knew who lived in Bushton. I'm thankful for that small town grapevine that protected me."

Being introduced to loving, caring adults "like the parents of my school classmates" was important to Linda. She mentioned that when she was still in elementary school, the local banker phoned our mother to suggest that our folks add her name to their checking account because she had written and signed a "counter" check to pay for her school lunches. "Where else but in a small town would a banker (William Volkland) handle such a minor matter in such a personal way?"

She also wondered "where else but in a small town would a high school math and science teacher (Jim Tiner) come to the home of a student several nights in a row to sit at the kitchen table and tutor a student who was recovering from surgery?" Linda was that student.

Lanara Luthi had similar recollections about trust and freedom. "We knew everyone in town and where they lived," she said. "We called every adult 'Mr. or Mrs. and didn't use a casual address out of respect."

She said "kids enjoyed a lot of freedom. We could walk or ride bikes anywhere in town. We roller skated anywhere but mostly in front of the church because the sidewalks were the smoothest in town. She said the sidewalks in front of many homes were rough because of tree roots. "Sometimes," she said, "even walking could be hazardous."

The trust and freedom experienced by young people in

those days was not unusual in small towns like Bushton.

Sue (Habiger) Dahlsten also feels she grew up in the best of times. "None of the families had much money," she said, "but we had everything we needed." Sue tells people she grew up in a "little Utopia." But," she says, "it wasn't until I got to college that I realized everyone didn't grow up the way I did. There was always so much love and support in our family."

Ally's grandmother Dola Groth and our daughter Suzy in the mid-1960s.

Chapter 9

Not All Was Well in Rural Kansas

Down a country road…

ALL WAS NOT PERFECT in Bushton. The pastoral and peaceful life that many of us remember so fondly was not shared by everyone.

As I read a letter from Bonnie (Gregory) Housley ('58) I was saddened to think that I, and most of the rest of us, I'm sure, had no idea of the kind of life she led. Perhaps there were others whose lives were similar to hers. If so, I didn't know about them and they have not felt the need to tell their stories. Bonnie is very brave to have written me about her life and she has done a great favor to all of us who grew up in that time. I admire her greatly. Ally and I are terribly upset to learn about her circumstances, but what she has told us should help to at least somewhat balance the memories of those of us whose lives were richer and more meaningful.

Bonnie has given me permission to use her name and to tell her story. I'll let her do it. Following is the letter as she sent it to me, verbatim. She gave her permission to reprint it.

> Here is my account of growing up "rural." I'm not too sure you will want to use it. If not, just toss it. It's not very uplifting, but it is an honest account from a long time ago. If you do use it, feel free to use my name.
>
> There was a time when I was in school that I wouldn't talk of our life because I was too embarrassed about the way we lived, but I am long past that now. My life has been great; and the past is the past.

I grew up on the farm, the oldest of four children and the only girl. The first farm we lived on when I was small was near Pollard. My first and second grades were in a one-room school with outdoor privies. Can you imagine teaching all eight grades? I then attended Fairplay School on Highway 14 for four years. It had two rooms – and bathrooms!

We then moved to a farm near Frederick [*a small town six or so miles east of Bushton*] where I began 7th grade in Bushton. Imagine a room for each grade! This was about the time I began to realize the reality of our life and what would define me for the next six years.

My father was a tyrant who ruled his family with an iron hand. One of his favorite sayings was "You have kids to work, and if they don't work, they don't deserve to eat." And work we did! Every morning and evening there were many chores, which we did while he laid on the couch. When we weren't in school, he assigned us jobs to do while he went fishing. These could be fixing fences which were always broken down, shoveling out the barn or chicken house and spreading it on the fields, chopping tall weeds for the pigs to eat, hoeing and debugging and digging about an acre of potatoes, working in the huge garden or a myriad of other tasks that never seemed to run out. It was never done to his satisfaction. Mostly all this fell on Arlen, my oldest brother, and me. Since I was the only girl, I also had to help my mother in the house.

I hated everything about the farm, from the ramshackle house with no indoor plumbing to the blazing hot summers, the freezing cold winters, the constant wind that blew dust through the cracks, wearing other people's hand-me-down clothes, the constant criticism and the endless work that was never done.

The only relief from all this was school. I absolutely LOVED school. It was the one area where I excelled and felt equal or even superior to others. I was the ultimate teacher's pet, because I tried so hard to please.

We finally left the farm the spring of my senior year when my father took a job as manager of the grain elevator in Frederick. I knew there was no way I could go to college, despite my good grades. I did, however, manage a year at Fort Hays State College. They offered a one-year business course. Of course, I had to pay him [*her father*] back for that.

When I finished at Hays, I got a job and moved to Hutchinson. I loved living in the city, supporting myself and not having to answer to anyone. It was wonderful! It was during this time that I met my husband; and shortly after we got married we moved to his hometown of Van Buren, Arkansas. I have been there ever since. It's the perfect size small city with the larger city of Fort Smith just across the Arkansas River.

Bob is the opposite of my father. He is kind, easy going and absolutely adores his children and grandchildren. Our son and his wife live in Denver. Our daughter and her husband and two college-age children live here in Van Buren, although both kids are away at college. It's been wonderful watching the grandkids grow up.

As you might surmise, I have absolutely no nostalgia for the "rural" life or the "good old days." Would I feel differently if our home life hadn't been so difficult? I don't know – maybe. The main thing, the years since have been wonderful, and the past is just that – the past. I'm beyond thankful for the life I have now, and I can't see dwelling on something that happened long ago.

Thank you for sharing that, Bonnie. If you hadn't written it, this Memoir would not have been complete. I'm sure that all who read this are happy that your life has turned out so well and that you are happy and fulfilled. And I am personally delighted that you have been able to put the past behind you and enjoy the life you now have. (LKM)

Doctors have found that constant stress can change the

chemistry in a child's brain. Stress, they say, is triggered by a physiological reaction and is the consequence of adrenaline and other hormones flooding our system.

Bonnie obviously dealt with childhood trauma in such a positive manner that she has been able to put it behind her and focus on the good life she now has. She took to heart Charles Dickens' plea that everyone should "reflect upon your present blessings, of which every man [*and woman*] has many – not on your past misfortunes, of which all men [*and women*] have some.

I wish there had been more "fun" in Bonnie's growing up years.

*Bonnie (Gregory) Housley ('58)
and her husband Bob*

Chapter 10

A Rock in the Rear and 8mm Film

Down a country road…

SPEAKING OF FUN: while I was growing up in Bushton there wasn't a lot of entertainment. There probably still isn't. "To see a movie you went to Holyrood, Lyons or Great Bend," Dale Nordstrom said. But, he reminded me as did several others so it must have been important to many, that in the summer we had free outdoor movies.

Jalayne Clark recalls that a couple from Chase, another small town a dozen or so miles south and east of Bushton, brought a projector and screen to town every other Saturday night and showed movies in an area between the baseball and football fields. "Most people sat on blankets, a few on chairs and some in their cars." She believes local businesses paid for the expense of bringing the films and screening them.

Rita (McKay) Hamman ('60) said she, her sister Wanda ('61) and other friends, always went early with their blankets so "we could get a good spot. Our parents went later and parked the car behind those on blankets and lawn chairs. They often watched the movie from the car."

"Nearly everyone in town showed up, even out-of-town people," said Jo (Lindsay) Hodges.

Lanara Luthi said she remembers cowboy movies and continuing serials in which the hero was always left hanging from a cliff or some other dangerous position at the end of each episode."

"You brought your own seating and refreshments," Dale Nordstrom said.

He also recalled that "a circus came to town one time and

erected a tent west of the school." He remembered a performance in the school gymnasium by the "Rangers Quartet" who sang gospel songs and sold records. "Other than that," he said, "you were on your own."

Ally and I always managed to sit together at the free outdoor movies. Ever try to sit stiff-backed for two hours with your arm around a pretty blue-eyed girl while a rock (always a pointed one, it seemed) poked painfully into your rump through a blanket? I don't recall much about the movies but the discomfort (for two hours or so) was certainly worth it. I hope it was worth it for her, too. Actually, I had put my arm around Ally for the first time in the single row of seats in the balcony of the Holyrood movie theatre. I have no idea how I mustered up the courage to do so, but somehow I did. I don't remember what the movie was or even how she reacted – to the movie or to my arm around her shoulders. I assume it was okay as I think I left it around her for the entire film. My arm ached and finally went numb, but, so what?

I think it cost 15 or 20 cents to see a movie in those days although Myretta thinks it was 50 cents.

Ally's brother Wayne found other opportunities for entertainment.

Wayne Groth and his horse Midge.

He recalled a Christmas that opened up some new worlds for him. "Christmas was always a special occasion with plenty of presents and candy," he said. "I never seemed to get the electric train that I wished for but I was well taken care of with other gifts." A "special time" was the year a horse called Midge arrived at the Groth farm. "I can still recall the first ride on that horse and I have no idea how I was able to stay in the saddle as Midge took off at full speed," he said. "I spent a lot of time on that horse traveling the pasture and once in a while making the big trip to Bushton or Frederick."

Some fun! And Wayne is the only one of all the Bushton graduates with whom I visited or corresponded who mentioned horseback riding as entertainment.

Rita Hammond didn't have a horse as far as I know but found other ways to have fun. A taffy pull was one of those ways. At the Volkland's "Effie Volkland cooked the syrup to the right temperature, buttered our hands, then gave us each some very hot taffy to begin pulling. We had to be sure our hands were clean or the taffy would be gray."

Rita said there were seven kids on her block who were all about the same age. "On summer evenings," she said, "additional kids would come and we played softball until dark in the Weatherbee's side yard." She also mentioned slumber parties at Jane Shulz's farm where the hay loft became off limits "after we destroyed or damaged several bales of hay by jumping on them."

As a young boy, Fran Habiger built a tree house and then "a fort in the trees behind the house." He said because of living on a farm "I had lots of material to work with and I must have had a wide-ranging imagination."

Before TV was common to almost every household "women crocheted or knitted," Myretta Bell said. "Lots of folks had crocheted tablecloths, armchair covers and doilies under plants, lamps or other items. My mother had an ecru crocheted coverlet for our guest bed over a coral satin floor length underskirt."

She also mentioned radio station XERF, "the border blaster from over the border" in Mexico. "On date night," she said, "XERF played all our songs. They were love songs, not hate raps." The singers she mentioned included Pat Boone, Dean Martin, Frank Sinatra, Perry Como, Patti Page and Doris Day. "It was rumored," she said, "the station reached all the way up to Canada on a cold winter night." She said she never did order their genuine faux diamond ring for $2.98.

Jo Hodges and her family worked hard to create opportunities for entertainment. Her father worked for Northern Natural Gas Company (on various night and day shifts). "When he came home from work on his daytime shift we gathered up all the kids on the block and played softball," she said.

Jo and her three siblings made their own toys. "Boys made cars and girls made dolls. Sometimes we played grown-up with high heels made of sticks." She said when she was older she and her sister made paper doll clothes out of wall paper sample books they received from the local hardware store. "We also had roller skates and one bicycle the three of us shared."

As an aside, Jo said she hated her name. "All the boys teased me unmercifully about having a boy's name." She said her mother tried to make her feel better by telling her the name came from the movie *Little Women*. "I still didn't feel good about it," she said, "until I moved to California where there were a lot of women my age named Jo."

Personally, I never gave her name a second thought. Actually, I like it.

Others, including Fran Habiger, found entertainment in the great outdoors by hunting and fishing. Fran said he went often. "I just loved to walk along the creek and take in Mother Nature," he said.

"Hoot" felt the same. He remembered shooting jack rabbits and fishing the creeks. He enjoyed hunting pheasants and said "there was even a squirrel season."

But hunting and fishing weren't just for the males. Millie Sanderson said her Thanksgiving days were spent hunting in the morning with her father. For dinner they had whatever game the hunter and huntress brought the wife and mother.

"I did become a good shooter," Millie said. "A gun was used for getting food."

She said she learned to fish in the creek not far from her first house in Bushton. "I cleaned the fish I caught," she said, "and today I still enjoy eating catfish."

Several Bushton grads mentioned being a member of the high school band and getting to march in parades such as at the annual State Fair in Hutchinson.

Lanara Luthi said that in the early fall "the school band would practice their marching drills on the streets of town, learning to turn corners and reverse march while preparing for the Hoisington Labor Day Parade and the State Fair." She said mothers and little kids came out to the curbside to listen and watch.

The school purchased band uniforms, said Marilyn Wilkens ('56), "but cheerleading outfits my junior and senior year were our responsibility." She said her parents bought the material and she made her own uniform.

"Sewing was a big part of our summer," she said. "The first Sunday dress I made was for Easter when I was 12, and the next year I made my 8th grade graduation dress." Marilyn said feedsack dresses that her mother sewed when she was younger were finally a thing of the past and the only time she sewed with feedsacks "was for our picnic tablecloth." She also said they embroidered "days of the week" tea towels and pillow cases finished with lace edging.

Perhaps it doesn't qualify as "fun" for some of the population but I suspect it was GREAT fun for some. I'm speaking of the phone system in and around Bushton. Almost everyone had a "party line."

That meant listening in to the conversations of other folks. Because so many of my classmates mentioned "party lines," listening in must have been a common occurrence.

Lanara said there was no dialing of numbers. "You would just wind the handle on the side of the wooden box with the speaker coming out of the front and the ear piece hanging on the side." The "operator" answered with "number please." Lanara said the Ostrander number was 146. "How did I remember that?" she wondered.

Sue Dahlsten and her brother Fran both recalled party line stories. When Fran and his wife Nancy lived in the town of Beeler, Kansas, the phone operator was named Beulah. Fran said his father called one day and Beulah told him Fran and Nancy were gone, she had just seen them leave. "Only in a small town does a stranger tell you the party you want on the phone is not at home," Fran said.

Sue said everyone "had a certain ring that was theirs. We had a long and two shorts," she said. "Everyone on your party line could listen to your conversation. When you were through talking you could just hear the receivers click down from people who had been listening."

Wayne Groth said his family's distinct ring was one long and three shorts. "Every home could hear each other's ring so you had to assume there were others listening to your phone call." The Groth family phone number, imprinted in Ally's mind, was 65F13.

Wayne said the phone system was maintained by a group of about a dozen farmers. "When there was a bad storm everyone got together and looked for telephone lines that needed to be repaired." He said it wasn't a fancy system and the poles supporting the lines looked like dead trees that were fairly straight. "When we finally got a dial phone at the farm we thought we had really modernized," he said.

"Living in a rural community you realize there aren't many secrets." Wayne said one can't be anonymous and you're recognized by everyone so if you say something inappropriate, those you care about are bound to find out. "I guess that is a good motivator to conduct yourself properly at all times," he said.

At least once I had to use the old phone in Ally's farmhouse (a phone we still have as a fond remembrance). I had to call my parents to tell them I would be late getting home for one reason or another. I think it cost 10 cents to call from the farm to Bushton. I'm not sure I ever paid her parents for the use of the phone and the fact that I didn't still bothers me. I don't think her folks worried about it, though.

* * * *

In 1953, when I was in the 8th grade, my Dad bought an 8mm movie camera. It seemed from that moment on he was never without it, or a newer one. There was seldom an event in Bushton (at least one in which my sister and/or I were involved) that wasn't recorded on film. Not long ago, because I owned a video production company and had the equipment, I transferred most of that 8mm film to, first, VHS tape and then, later, to DVD. It has been wonderful, in that way, to relive much of my growing-up years.

Because Ally and I found each other early in life, there is lots of footage of her, too. Thanks, Dad.

It was more or less natural for my Dad to have a camera, movie or still, with him almost all the time. He had four brothers, three of whom were professional portrait photographers. We've got several portraits of my folks, my sister and me thanks to those uncles of mine

Thinking back, I recall much of my growing-up life as a series of short film clips.

I am riding my bike out of the yard of our first house in Bushton. Cut to me crossing the railroad tracks (a rough crossing). I suspect I was on my way to school because the next cut is to me riding down the town's Main Street. There are a few cars parked in the center of the wide unpaved street. Fewer still were parked against the curbs. Cut to me parking my bike in front of the school.

Here I'm using the old scissor kick in high jumping competition at a 1953 track meet in Sterling. (Thanks to Russell Vail for the photo)

There is black and white film of the 1953 grade school track meet at Sterling College. It might be the first film my Dad ever shot. Lots of adults I recognize, mainly parents of young athletes, cheerleaders and other students. There is a relay race. When I take the handoff from the first runner (maybe it was

Eugene Hoelscher ('57) I am in first place. When I hand it off, maybe to Phil Henry ('57), I am in third place. Obviously, I was not a particularly fast runner. I think our team ended up in second place, thanks to a speedy Russell Vail ('59) who anchored the team. Maybe it was third. We didn't seem to mind. Cut to me, Phil and the others laughing with our arms around each other.

Cut to a color sequence of my sister Linda and her close friend Joan Moege running around and around a good-size lilac bush in our front yard. Perhaps my Dad, the photographer, told them to move. "This is motion pictures," he might have said. They ran.

Cut to an all-school picnic where nearly everyone in town and most of the outlying farmers and their families show up. I recognize most of them although I don't remember all their names. They line up for a buffet. Many sit in the shade against a wall of the school. Lots of cuts to one person, families, kids, food.

My 8th grade graduation at which I sang in the "Janitor Boys" Quartet. It included, from left, me, Nathan Kelly, Phil Henry and Darrol Timmons, a 7th grader who was also a janitor that year.

Lawrence Timmons (more on him later), our 8th grade teacher and elementary school principal, always saw to it that there was an elaborate graduation ceremony for the 8th graders who were headed off to high school (there was no middle school in those days). Cut to scenes of that event. We were all dressed up. The girls wore billowing skirts and the boys wore coats and ties. Cut to me singing in a "men's" quartet. I sang because Ally thought I should. She and Jeanne (Volkland) Huebner (both a year behind me) played *Pomp and Circumstance* on two pianos. I think Ally cried because I was "graduating." In fact, Lanara Luthi said, recalling those ceremonies, both grade school and high school, that "*Pomp and Circumstance* still brings little tears to my eyes."

Cut to sequences of the Bushton Study Club, with my folks, Ally's parents and many others having a special dinner out at the famous fried chicken restaurant in Brookville, Kansas, playing bingo, having a Halloween party at Coach Winter's and a picnic in Volkland's yard.

Brookville was near Salina, perhaps an hour's drive northeast of Bushton, and people went there from throughout the state to sample their famous fare and to enjoy an evening out with friends.

Cut to a brief shot of Ally riding my bike. That bike holds great memories for me. My parents bought it for me while we lived in Russell and I will never forget how proud I was of it and the resulting freedom it signified. It was a red Schwinn and had two crossbars (a boy's bike had them, girls bikes did not) one above the other, between the handle bars and the seat. A special memory (although not on film – I hope) was when I was taking Ally to her grandmother's house from our home on the wrong side of the tracks. She rode, probably very uncomfortably (especially across the railroad tracks), kind of side-saddle on those crossbars. I must have not yet been 16 and had no driver's license. I remember stopping in front of Miss Holland's house, next door to Grandma Groth's, helping Ally off the bike and kissing her for the first time. I don't remember anything else about that evening. Not walking her to the door. Not riding back across the railroad tracks to get home. Nothing else. Nothing else mattered.

I think of that often when I see a plaque in my daughter Suzy's house, no doubt placed there by Denny, her husband. "We were together," it reads. "I forget the rest." It's a quote by Walt

Whitman.

Speaking of bike-riding: many of my classmates talked about the freedom they felt when riding their bicycles, as well as the trust their parents showed by letting them ride freely just about wherever they wanted.

Millie Sanderson, for example, said her bike "opened up another world to me." She could ride into town from her farm and see school friends. "Most of the time I got into trouble," she said, "because I had not told anyone where I was going." She said she had a bike that looked like the witch's bike from *The Wizard of Oz*. She said she rode to get fresh milk from a farmer south of town and to her cousin Dale Nordstrom's house to use his World Books. She also rode to the library "which I loved" and where she read all the Nancy Drew and Hardy Boys books "and everything else they had on the shelves."

My bicycle got me to and from wherever I wanted or needed to go in those days. In fact, I both wanted and needed to visit Ally on many Saturdays and I pedaled that bike (the typical old Schwinn with no gears and "iffy" brakes) five miles on a mostly gravel road on many Saturdays because she had a big black and white TV set that brought in a football game which she graciously watched with me. I'm not sure at all that she enjoyed the games. I did enjoy the games but, perhaps more than that, I enjoyed sitting beside her to watch them.

I don't recall being bothered, or even winded, by riding that old bike for five miles on a largely unpaved road. But it surely must have been more difficult than today's bicycle riders have it on their expensive, lightweight, ten-geared (or more) bikes.

Cut to scenes of Neil Denton, me and other Boy Scouts with Mr. Timmons giving instructions, setting up a camp with many small tents.

Cut to me and Nathan Kelly, a classmate who moved from town long before our class graduated, with arms around each other in the summer of 1953 as we prepared to depart on a trip to St. Louis which we had won in some kind of contest of which I have no recollection.

*Me and Nathan Kelly as we prepared to leave
on the trip we won to St. Louis in 1953.*

We saw the St. Louis Browns play the Yankees on that trip with hundreds of other contest winners from, I suspect, throughout the Midwest. We all shouted, toward the end of the game when the Yankees were way ahead, that "We Want Satchel!" In response, the Browns' manager let Satchel Paige pitch for an inning. It was probably one of his last appearances there although he was, probably as an honor, named to the All-Star team that year which was the Browns' last in St. Louis. They lost 100 games that year and then moved to Baltimore and became the Orioles. Attendance at their last game was 3,174.

But we got to see a major league baseball game. I should have taken Dad's movie camera with me.

Dad took pains to film the businesses, the bank, library and other buildings and people on Main Street. There is Delbert Henry and son Joe exiting the Bushton Drugstore, there is Cecil Dalzel in front of his barbershop, Ed Habiger in town on some kind of business, others as well. There is film of our first house in Bushton – the one on the wrong side of the tracks – and sequences of the surrounding flat farmland.

There are other brief film clips that I remember as though the events were yesterday.

Playing baseball on our vacant lot. The football letterman's banquet. An oil well and pumping unit filmed by my Dad – a natural sight in those days. Wheat harvest with Ally's Dad Vernon driving the combine. Another community picnic, this one put on by the grain elevator folks. Football practice with me getting back in line after hitting the tackling dummy and blowing a bubble. I note there are no face masks on the helmets. A baseball game in which I'm the pitcher. Linda Byers and Rita Hammon pulling a small wagon (maybe it had soft drinks in it) toward a baseball game. Linda and Carol Koonce, our cousin from Oklahoma, washing the '52 Studebaker. Lots of video of vacation trips to Colorado or Oklahoma. Lots of film of aunts and uncles and my parents visiting the cemetery in Bokoshe, Oklahoma (nearly in Arkansas), where my grandmother Williams is buried. A series of Christmases including one with Santa Claus riding a flatbed truck down Bushton's Main Street with what seemed like a large crowd in those days. Methodist church-goers leaving the building after Sunday morning services and pausing on the steps to be filmed. Everyone is dressed in their Sunday best. They smile at the camera. Grainy black and white film of basketball games featuring me, Lyle Komarek ('58), Phil Henry, the Huebner twins (Ray and Jay – both '57) and others, of course. Shoveling snow in front of our "old" house and later from the sidewalk in front of the "new" house. Ally hitting a practice golf ball and pointing like she'd just hit a home run. Wayne astride his horse Midge on the street near our house. A picnic in our backyard with me and Ally, Neil, Fran, Gary Prosser ('57), Phil, cousin Carol, Sue Dahlsten and Shirley Mullenix.

  I mentioned earlier that both my parents were part of large families. All of those living aunts and uncles from both the Meredith and Williams branches were filmed (a great deal, it seems) by my father.

  I think we went to Colorado – to the valley where Ally and I, our children and grandchildren now live – every summer for my Dad's vacation. Three of Dad's brothers lived there, or nearby, and we always enjoyed our time with hordes of uncles, aunts and boy and girl cousins. Dad's three brothers who lived in Colorado were all congenial men with outstanding senses of humor whom I liked and admired. As I recall, they all liked their bourbon and my Uncle Pegg (Lowell Meredith) made what he called "black Russian" drinks. My cousin Bob (the son of Lowell and Ione) became a close friend and even a business partner in a venture that was amiable and fun. I see and hear from other Colorado cousins now and then. Bob, in the meantime, bought a boat and, with his wife Trish, planned to sail around the world. They got as far as Guatemala where they now live fulltime. They used to get back to Colorado occasionally to visit Trish's mother in Fruita, Colorado, or her daughter Ty who now lives in Washington state.

We also made trips to Oklahoma to see Dad's sister Lorene and her family which included the aforementioned Carol. That was in my hometown of Chandler but the town wasn't like Bushton and I was always glad to get home.

Mother's side of the family consisted mainly, it seemed, of sisters and Uncle Bill. We have lots of film of the sisters in Bokoshe visiting the cemetery on Memorial Day. I think my uncle Bill (H.G. Williams of Wichita) and his wife Opal made sure all the sisters got to make that trip on a regular basis.

In the film everyone is standing in a group, self-consciously looking at the cameraman. The men put their arms around the women all of whom wear dresses and hats. They clutch at their skirt hems, trying to hold them down in the wind. Their purses flap at their slides. Hats are askew. Aunt Opal blows a kiss at the camera and shows sunburn on her shoulder. Everyone looks at the tombstones. Uncle Bill takes off his suitcoat. His dress shirt glares like a white hot sun at the camera. Two or three cars line the cemetery's streets. They are late '50s models, maybe a '61. Suddenly the image cuts harshly to black and white film of a high school basketball game. The aunts and uncles are gone.

I loved the aunts but was in awe of them. There were Ruby, Ruth, Mabel and Stella, and my mother Eva. We called Ruth "Aunt Poody" for some reason. She got a great kick out of frightening the youngsters during the night. Ruby was the serious one. One of her sons died in a submarine in WWII. Mabel was the funny one who found humor in just about anything. I didn't know Aunt Stella very well. She and her husband lived in Oregon before he died. She then moved to Tulsa where the other sisters lived. She was very serious and, I think, not very tolerant of children. Her shiny black hair encased her head like a helmet. I liked her but was wary of her. I'm glad they all continue to live on in Dad's movie film. There are other distant relatives, too. Most of them show up on film at one time or another. Most, like the sisters, are no longer living.

There is more. Thank God there is more. Friends are shown as youngsters, adults much younger than I am now (most gone), vacation trips to the mountains or to cities which were interesting but which we couldn't wait to leave and return to our little town.

There is much film of our town shot from the top of the grain elevator in 1954 showing the wide unpaved Main Street. How small Bushton was and still is. The 9-hole golf course with sand greens where many of us learned to drive a golfball is pictured. I still don't know how Dad got permission to go to the top of the elevator or how he got there.

And, though it has nothing to do with Bushton, there is film of me and my family riding the ski lift at Aspen, Colorado, one summer in the rain. It is the famous old Lift No. 1, a single chair that carried us to the summit of Aspen Mountain which Ally and I would later ski down and which our Son Greg and his son Jack have skied regularly. Our granddaughter Lauren is also a skier and, we hope, a careful one. Visible in the background are other surrounding ski mountains where our children learned to ski at an early age.

My sister and I cherish those old films. My Dad kept on filming until his death in 1990. Again, thanks Dad.

Dad with one of his movie cameras.

Our grandchildren Jack and Lauren

134 – REAL, RURAL

CHAPTER 11

That Old Work Ethic

Down a country road lies…

EVEN WITH ALL THAT going on we were learning to work.

Our role models were our parents, most of the other adults in and around the town, our school teachers, our Sunday school teachers, other religious and academic leaders and even older students.

I've written about my Dad who was a wonderful role model. He worked hard, complimented me when I did well on whatever job I tried whether it was bagging groceries, mowing lawns or actually working for him. He never complained. He took on the hard jobs without a whimper and worked until the job was finished—and finished right. I've tried to model my worklife after his. I hope it has measured up.

And there were others, too.

Let's talk first about Lawrence Timmons. I told you there would be more about him.

He was the elementary school principal, 8th grade teacher, coach of all elementary grade boys' sports teams, acting custodian for the grade school, cafeteria manager, scout leader and leader of whatever else needed a leader.

He was tough (at least he *seemed* tough) and we trusted, respected and sometimes feared him. He was a little man (he wasn't very tall) but he lived large. It was that way from the beginning of Mr. Timmons' career in education.

Darrol Timmons said his father married Ruby June Collinge in 1927 after getting permission from their parents because they were both under the age of 21. They had just graduated from Geneseo High School – another small town 15 miles east of Bushton – and that same year Mr. Timmons took a job as the lone teacher at a country grade school near Crawford, Kansas,

Darrol said his father's first students included two 16-year-old boys who claimed responsibility for driving away their previous teacher. "They stated that they intended to get rid of him also," Darrol said. These two insisted the only way they would listen to him was "if he could whip both of them." Mr. Timmons accepted the challenge but said they had to fight him one at a time. "My dad had grown up with four brothers," Darrol said, "and he was convinced he could prevail."

He did.

After that, Darrol said, the three of them got along well. "In fact they continued to be in touch after the boys received their diplomas."

Mr. Timmons was a worker. Darrol said he learned his work ethic at a young age "following my Dad around as he performed cleaning and fixit tasks in the school building and around the school grounds." As Darrol grew older his father increasingly gave him more tasks to do, "finally including mowing the school yard and driving the small tractor to 'drag' the dirt infield of the baseball field."

Darrol said when he finally entered high school he lost interest in the janitorial job offered by his Dad "in favor of paying farm jobs like driving a grain truck from the harvest field to elevator, stacking hay bales on a trailer behind a hay bailer, then hauling the hay to a barn for storage." When nothing else was available Darrol would take a job "driving a tractor, pulling a four-bottom plow all day long" which he found very boring but which "gave me the money to buy gas for my '53 Ford."

A few of the 8th grade boys, including me, each year got the "honor" from Mr. Timmons of being "janitor boys." That meant we stayed after school to push mops around the floors of the hallways and classrooms and generally clean up the place. It didn't take long and, as I recall, we were paid a little for our efforts. Mr. Timmons, like Tom Sawyer, made the work seem like an honor. What a great role model. Other than mowing lawns with our small gasoline-powered mower, that was my real introduction to the workplace with a supervisor hovering around making sure the job was done properly. I remember taking a gallon gasoline can to the gas station downtown with a quarter and filling the can with fuel for the mower.

Later, my work life included jobs on farms, bagging groceries and working at Northern Natural which was a kind of rite of passage for Bushton boys. At Northern I was once assigned the filthiest job at the plant – cleaning the pistons. That meant scraping the black soot-like carbon off the pistons and realizing that most of it ended up on me and my clothes. In fact, I was so filthy at the end of the day that Neil Denton, who gave me a ride to and from work that summer, made me ride home at the end of that workday in the trunk of his car.

One summer I worked with my Dad at Jones and Laughlin Supply Company's store in Chase (a few miles southeast of Bushton). I swept the floor, "goosed" the weeds in the pipeyard and delivered parts and equipment to pumping units, drilling rigs and pulling units throughout the center of the state.

Often Dad gave me directions to the rig that needed the parts. He'd say something like: "go down the highway about 20 or 25 miles and there's a big cottonwood tree, turn left onto the county road there and go a ways until you come to a farmhouse with a mailbox that looks like a birdcage. Just past that farmhouse is a bridge over a creek – it'll probably be dry – and within 50 or a hundred yards is two-track road that runs off to the left into a pasture toward a drilling rig. That's where you're going." Somehow I always found my destination out there in the vast flatland where county roads divide up the prairie into one-mile-square segments that all look the same.

I seemed to make those deliveries quickly, too. There was an older man who worked at the Chase store and often made the deliveries. Call him Carl. I don't recall if that was his name or not. According to the other men at the store, Carl always took twice as long as I did in making the deliveries. Go figure.

Another summer I worked for my uncle Willis Koonce in Chandler, Oklahoma. He owned a furniture and appliance store and had a plumbing business on the side. Mainly, I helped the plumber. He was another older man whose name I've also forgotten. Let's call him Fred. Fred and I were under maybe half the homes in Chandler that summer, fixing broken pipes, adding water lines, doing other various plumbing jobs and trying to avoid centipedes. Without his realizing it, Fred taught me how to swear. I think he knew, and I learned, every swearword in existence – and he may have invented a few more.

There was this hill on the north side of town. The street ran down the hill west, across the railroad tracks and into a sharp curve north out toward the Turner Turnpike. I was driving the company pickup one day and, as we started down that hill, the brakes failed. The truck rapidly picked up speed and we bounced crazily across the railroad tracks and careened madly around the curve. As we did so, pipe and tools bounced out of the bed of the truck and scattered noisily all over the street. I was finally able to bring the truck to a halt by down-shifting and letting it coast. That was the only time I ever saw Fred speechless. A mouthful of swearwords surely must have gathered in his throat and gagged him.

When our daughter Suzy and her husband Denny lived in Tulsa we made a trip to Chandler. That majestic hill didn't seem quite as steep as I remembered it.

While there, by the way, we visited the old Armory from which my Dad left for World War II. It has been converted into the Route 66 Interpretive Center which is quite well done and interesting. It's a huge red-stone building that looks like a fortress or a low-slung castle.

I also recall that Phil Henry and I once spent an entire day cleaning and organizing the steaming hot attic of the Bushton Mercantile Store and were paid the total of a watermelon each. We thought it was great.

How young and naïve we were. But we were learning to work.

Don "Hoot" Hiltbrunner said in those days "fathers went to work, mothers stayed home." Don said he worked in the Nelson Hardware store during 8th grade and the following summer "sorting, cleaning and assisting the owner's son with furnace installations." The son, Don said, had been a glider pilot during the Normandy invasion which helped bring WWII closer to an end. "The upstairs area was full of working horse collars left over from those days of farming with horses," Don said. He was paid "with a Remington .22 rifle in lieu of cash." He still has it.

Neil Denton recalled that one summer he and Hoot were working on farms that were nearly adjacent to each other (one was Ally's father's) and the farmers decided they both needed their barnyards cleaned up. Neil and Hoot, they decided, should team up.

The two shoveled loads of manure onto trailers to be spread on fields as fertilizer. Working together, they passed each other as they made their rounds in the fields and began throwing manure at each other. How it started or who initiated it is not known but, Neil said, they had a great time.

During his freshman year, Hoot said, "Harry Groth brought me into his Chevrolet store."

Dola and Harry Groth, Ally's grandparents. Harry owned a Chevy/Oldsmobile dealership and Don Hiltbrunner worked there while in high school.

Harry Groth was Ally's grandfather who owned a Chevrolet-Oldsmobile dealership. Hoot said "it was a very, very sad day in May of 1954 when Harry was killed in a car accident. It was a great loss for Bushton." It was a great loss for the Groth family as well. Ally had been very close to Harry and her grandmother Dola and the trauma she felt at his death was felt by all of us in that small town. At that time Ally and I were by then considered a "couple."

Recalling his time with the Groth Motor Company, "Hoot" said "Frank Fidler and another older mechanic who lived in a small trailer house beside the store, taught me how to do a lube, oil and filter change, how to tune a car engine and change tires. I was the gopher," Hoot said, "cleaning the place, organizing the parts room, helping the mechanics, washing cars and doing other, similar, jobs." He said he drove Harry home from work and picked him up the next morning "in his red 1938 Ford pickup which I parked in front of my house at night."

I didn't know Harry Groth well but I do remember now and then having lunch with him and Dola and always after lunch, Harry announced he would "show you a trick." He then lay down on the sofa and took a nap.

Like most of us, "Hoot" also did farm work as a young man. He appreciated "being taken under the wing of a farmer who trained you to operate his expensive farm equipment while paying you $5.00 a day and room and board during the summer." Hoot said he learned "to work the fields and maintain the farm" and that "being turned loose driving a Case tractor with a plow was a first step into manhood." He said his job included "working the baled hay, stacking it on the trailer or in the barn with a hayhook (which, he said, was a test of your being). Driving the wheat truck along with the combine as it was filled up and then driving it to the Bushton Elevator was a proud time. You literally became a family member, working the farm alone, milking the cow, gathering eggs while they went on vacation to New York."

Like "Hoot" and me, Darrol Timmons worked at several jobs during his growing-up years and, because he lived in a small rural town, the opportunities were limited. So he worked at much the same kind of jobs as did the rest of us. During the four summers of his undergraduate years at K-State Darrol worked at Northern Natural. "Three of those summers I worked as part of the compressor engine repair and overhaul crew," he said. "Because there were several operating engines in the same building where we were working, the summer afternoon inside temperatures became much too hot for comfort and for safety. Therefore, we were allowed to work a 6:00 a.m. to 2:30 p.m. shift instead of the usual 8:00 a.m. to 4:30 p.m. shift." This, he said, gave him the opportunity to work other jobs to earn money for college. "If the job was either during wheat harvest or in the hay field and needed to start before I could get there between 2:30 and 3:00 p.m. my Dad [*the aforementioned energetic Lawrence Timmons*] would frequently tag-team with me and perform the work until I arrived. Otherwise I would have to turn down the job. I also had two mowing jobs – a country school yard and a cemetery – which I could handle on Saturday." Like his father, Darrol seemed to be "working" all the time.

But it wasn't just the boys who worked. Despite what Myretta Bell said in Chapter 7 about there being few jobs for females in Bushton, women and young girls worked hard in many ways.

Shirley Mullenix said she loved mowing grass when she was in the 7th grade or higher, using an old-time reel push mower "until we could afford a better one."

Joy Nickerson, as mentioned earlier, worked in the drug store and some of her best memories "were getting to see so many happy faces at the soda fountain."

Many of the recollections of working on the part of young women revolved around the farm and the daily, often grueling, tasks they were assigned. On a farm, there was always something to be done and the young people were almost always involved.

Sue Dahlsten said when she was a Freshman in high school (while her brother Fran was a Junior and a younger brother Rob was a second grader) "my Mom had to go to the KU Med Center for surgery and Fran and I ran the farm for a few days while my folks were gone." This would not have been unusual for any farm family, she said. "The farm kids all knew how to milk the cows and take care of the livestock and were very responsible kids."

Millie Sanderson said her jobs were to "gather the eggs and put them in cases, get the coal from the shed and bring the bucket into the house, wash and dry the dishes with my sisters, take the peas from the pods, pick up the potatoes from the hills that my dad had dug up and get the cows up from the field with our dog." She also had to churn the cream to make butter and still has the cream can they used on the farm. She also has "the iron that we would heat in the fire and then pull it out to iron our clothes."

Marilyn Wilkens remembers when her mother wanted a fireplace/cookstove outside. "Dad built a wonderful brick one in the backyard," she said. "With the water heated in buckets, we were ready for up to ten chickens at a time." She described the process. "First, hanging by their feet from the clothesline to get their heads chopped off, then into the hot water, and off came the feathers. Sitting around the long picnic table, several of us cut up the chickens for the freezer." Usually, she said, there were two chickens to a package and "the record was 100 chickens a day." Clothes lines were always cleaned thoroughly before she hung out clothes.

"When the field of sweet corn was ready for us to pick and shuck," she said, "some of the same procedure was followed: Heat the water, blanch the corn, then go to the table to cut corn off the cob, spread onto cookie sheets to freeze and package later in stackable containers."

Ally, then known as Alyce Lyn, and now my wife of many wonderful years, had similar experiences growing up on a farm. She is to this day tough, energetic and a hard worker. In addition to the farm chores she was assigned, she was planning a career as a pianist and vocalist and, because of that, added to her days of work and study were hours of practice under the watchful eyes and encouragement of her mother and father, both musicians. It has paid off wonderfully.

My sister Linda also worked on a farm and had much the same experiences as recounted by other young women. She especially recalled living through the wheat harvests. "It was hot, sweaty work for the men in the fields," she said, "and it was the same for the farm wives roasting in their hot kitchens cooking meals for the men." She said women, men and some teenagers drove the wheat-laden farm trucks to town and lined up for blocks waiting their turns to deposit their wheat at the grain elevator where it would be checked and weighed." Linda said they waited in their hot trucks with the windows rolled down hoping to get a good price for their wheat.

Getting a "good" price for wheat in the 1950s was not

always easy. In fact, a *Grain and Feed Statistics Report* from the U.S. Department of Agriculture in 1965 shows that wheat prices per bushel actually fell from $2.13 in 1951 to $1.74 in 1960. The highest price per bushel, however, spiked to $2.18 in 1954 before falling again. Wheat production, measured in bushels per acre ranged from 13 to nearly 30, or maybe slightly more, in the 50s, depending on weather – rain or the lack of it, hail which could wipe out an entire crop in a matter of hours, heat and other factors. Wheat farmers and their families had to be optimistic folks who took whatever came with a stoic attitude and a hope that "wait'll next year" would see them through. Ally's family was happy and enthusiastic during the "good" years but I never saw them "down" when they had a less-than-hoped-for harvest.

Wheat, the Bushton area farmers' main crop, has a boom and bust kind of history. In the 1930s, for example, during the Depression and the Dust Bowl, many farmers were receiving less for their crop than its cost of production – a certain recipe for default and foreclosure. However, between 1871 and 1921 annual wheat production in the U.S. more than tripled. Herbert Hoover set a basic price of $2.20 for wheat during World War I. But by the end of the war prices fell to $1.01.

My father-in-law Vernon Groth, Ally's Dad, a Rice County farmer all his life, told me he had always looked forward to $5.00 wheat. When he retired from farming he had not seen that price.

But we were talking about how young people worked and/or learned to work in the 50s.

Our role models were basically the adults who made up the world around us – our parents, teachers, friends, business people, farmers, etc.

Lawrence Timmons seemed always to be working at one job or another, As mentioned, in school he was a one-man administration for the elementary school, a coach, a scout leader and a friend. Even his wife Ruby, Darrol's mom, set a positive example by serving as head cook in the school cafeteria for a decade.

For those of you who knew the Timmons family, Darrol reports that, after retiring in 1973, his parents moved to north-central Arkansas not far from the University of Missouri at Columbia where Darrol was on the faculty and where their two youngest grandchildren were. At that time Mr. Timmons was diagnosed with prostate cancer and had surgery. He was also diagnosed with macular degeneration but he continued to be typically active. Darrol says Mr. Timmons mentored eight more Eagle Scouts which brought the total Eagles he had mentored to 50.

"I have to emphasize the impact that Boy Scouts had on my life in Bushton," Darrol said. Starting out in Cub Scouts he soon graduated to Boy Scouts earning ranks from Tenderfoot to Eagle. In addition to camping and hiking at area scout camps he made three trips to the Philmont Scout Ranch in northeast New Mexico, two trips to National Boy Scout Jamborees in California and Pennsylvania and two trips to International Boy Scout Jamborees in Canada and England.

Some scenes from Boy Scouting with Mr. Timmons as Scoutmaster.

Mr. Timmons

Moms had to make sure all was well!

The Scout troop on a road trip. My Dad second from left, Mr. Timmons on far right.

Wayne Groth agreed that Scouting was important and "offered many opportunities for young lads" such as "new skills and camping experiences." Later, when his son Doug came of age, he became a Scoutmaster. "It made me realize that we probably didn't show enough appreciation for our Troop 175 Scoutmaster Lawrence Timmons," Wayne said. "He put a lot of effort into keeping the troop active for many years with quite a list of Eagle Scouts to add to his accomplishments."

Russell Vail who attended school in Bushton but ultimately graduated from Plains High School in 1959 is proud of the number of Eagle Scouts from Bushton who attained that honor largely through the mentorship of Lawrence Timmons. At a recent "All-School Reunion" (one is held every three years) in 2019, 13 of the 42 Eagle Scouts from Bushton were in attendance. Here's the list of all 42. I think it is appropriate to list their names in this book. Russell says he is, as far as he knows, the second oldest surviving Eagle Scout. The oldest is Darrol, the son of Mr. Timmons. Here are their names, the year they would graduate and the state in which they live (or if they are deceased) in no particular order:

    Karl A. Stehwein ('33) Deceased
    Harold Miller ('42) Deceased
    Darrol Timmons ('58) Washington
    Byron Buehler ('59) Deceased
    Russell Vail ('59) Michigan
    Douglas Volkland ('60) Kansas
    Jerold Wolford ('60) Missouri
    Bruce Buehler ('59) Tennessee
    Jack Hinzman ('60) Georgia
    Joe Henry ('60) Missouri
    L.E. Timmons (Scoutmaster) Deceased
    Gail Brunk (Deceased)
    Wayne Groth ('61) California
    Roger Corn ('61) Kansas
    Scott Behnke (deceased)
    Robert Habiger ('65) Colorado
    Joe Hanna ('64) Texas
    Clayton Mantz ('62) Kansas
    Jerry Smith (?)
    Michael J. Behnke ('76) Kansas
    John C. Bredfeldt ('65) Georgia
    Dennis Huebner ('64) Kansas
    Howard Behnke ('69) Kansas
    Lance Behnke ('70) Washington
    Robert "Bob" Cullison ('71) Washington
    Dennis Sidwell ('69) Kansas

Douglas Sidwell ('70) Kansas
James "Jim" Brown ('69) California
David Corn ('72) Deceased
DeWayne Walls ('67) Kansas
Allen Altenbaumer ('71) Deceased
Len Altenbaumer ('71) Kansas
Jeffrey Cullison ('74) Nebraska
Lennie Schwerdtfeger ('71) Michigan
Jon Appel ('75) Kansas
Robin Drumm ('74) Oklahoma
Brad Gfeller ('74) Deceased
Steven Springer ('75) Kansas
Kirk Mische ('74) Kansas
John Sturn ('76) Kansas
Keith Turnbull ('75) Minnesota
Randall Scott Cullison ('76) Iowa

Thirteen of the 42 Bushton Eagle Scouts mentored by Lawrence Timmons attended a recent all-school reunion They are, seated, from left: Joe Henry (Kansas City, MO), Dennis Huebner (Hays, KS), Doug Volkland (Pawnee Rock, KS), Keith Turnbull (Richfield, MN), Howard Behnke (Lyons, KS), Jack Hinzman (Mariotta, GA). Standing, from left:

Roger Corn (Ellsworth, KS), Mike Behnke (Bushton, KS), Robert Habiger (Littleton, CO), Darrol Timmons (Richland, WA), Russell Vail (White Lake, MI), John Sturn (Ellinwood, KS), Robin Drumm (Ponca City, OK).

Mr. Timmons died in 1997. Mrs. Timmons (Ruby) lived four more years and died while recovering from gall bladder rupture surgery only two and a half months from her 92nd birthday.

* * * *

Another Bushton High faculty member whose life has become, for Ally and me, the story of a man who, though very small in stature, stood very tall in the belief he could achieve great things, both as a teacher and as a leader. His name was Lyle Meredith (no relation) and he was our music teacher in high school. He mentored Ally as she grew into an outstanding musician whose piano skills have been inherited by our daughter Suzy who has been principal pianist for orchestras, a faculty member of a prep school and has played keyboard for many travelling Broadway musicals.

Lyle Meredith (pic scanned from yearbook)

Mr. Meredith died in 2015 in Dodge City, Kansas. He had joined the Navy before finishing high school, earned a college degree and began teaching. His obituary, printed in the *Dodge City Globe* said his career in public education took him from Lincolnville to Wilson to Bushton to Nickerson to Plainville and finally to Dodge City, all in Kansas. During that time he taught band, choir, senior English and Debate. His choirs gathered Superior honors at the Kansas State High School Activities Association state level for 20 consecutive years and with solos and ensembles too numerous to count.

A member of the professional Barbershop quartet "The Travelaires" he directed Barbershop Choruses in Hays and Dodge City. He also served two terms as President of the Kansas Music Educators Association and was a church choir director in Dodge City for 31 years. He retired from public education in 1987, then was the voice of the Dodge City Cowboy Band, a DJ for Kansas Public radio, gave private music lessons and worked part time at J C Penny's in Dodge City.

We knew he was good but, looking back, we didn't know just how good he was. He had a great and positive impact on Ally's life and on mine, too. He had to be good. His name was Meredith. . .

Other teachers that Ally and I regard as positive role models include Miss Ellis, who taught sixth grade; Miss Holland, our English teacher who guided all who would listen through the often bewildering world of the English language and who first acquainted me with the power of the written word; Deane Banker, a perfectionist who taught industrial arts (shop) and physical science; Arthur Harvey, the best Principal any school could have; our coach throughout high school Calvin Winter who also taught social science classes; and, of course, Jim Tiner, extraordinary teacher of science and math. I say "extraordinary" because he tried and, unfortunately, failed to teach me trigonometry when I told my parents I wanted to become a dentist I eventually went into journalism. Dad convinced an initially reluctant Mr. Tiner to instruct me in trig after school on many days. Years later, when I was on the administrative staff at Western Colorado University in Gunnison, Ally and I discovered that the Tiners, who had retired to a home in El Dorado, Kansas, had a vacation home in Gunnison where Mr. Tiner had, years earlier, earned a master's degree from Western. Jim Tiner was an avid fisherman and loved to fly fish for trout in the Gunnison and surrounding rivers. He and his wife Marjorie became good friends with us and we saw them frequently every summer until health problems meant they couldn't make the trip to Colorado. Joe Henry ('60) was a close friend of the Tiners and corresponded regularly with them.

* * * *

Death is a hard thing to deal with and, for most of us, it is something that we face too often when our parents, friends and relatives die. Or classmates. At least three of my class of only 12 have died since we graduated – Phil Henry, Gary Prosser and, most recently Ray Huebner, twin brother of Jay Huebner, another classmate.

When we were in grade school and I was the tallest in our class Phil Henry was a little guy with a great smile. He soon discovered the weight room and, by pumping iron regularly, created a sculpted body and muscles that became the envy of all of us. He grew taller than me and became an outstanding athlete. He died in 2012 in Joplin, Mo.

Phil and I were good friends. We once told our parents we wanted to ride our bikes into the countryside and camp for the night. In reality we planned to bike to Holyrood (seven miles north of Bushton) and meet two girls at the movie theatre. One of the girls was Ally, of course.

After the movie we did intend to "camp out." But in the midst of our biking to a potential camping spot a heavy rainstorm blew up. Phil and I found a dry and cozy barn and snuggled down for the night. In the middle of the night, however, I awoke and saw a car on the country road not far from the barn and its lights were flashing. Even in the darkness, I recognized my father's car. I flashed a flashlight beam back at him and Phil and I made our ways down to my father who took us back to Bushton.

My Dad never said a scolding word to either of us. I think he might have been amused. Still, he had gotten out of bed on a stormy night and had driven into the country looking for his son. I expected a lecture but it never came. But I learned something good that night that I've never forgotten. One knows when one has done something wrong and, sometimes, a lecture adds nothing meaningful to the experience.

I'll never forget the name of the film we saw that night. It was *Trouble Along the Way* starring John Wayne as a football coach. An appropriate title. I saw it again on television not long ago. It brought back great memories of that night.

Gary Prosser was a nearby neighbor of mine in Bushton. We grew up together and became good friends. He wasn't an athlete but was well-liked by everyone as far as I know. I can find no information about when or how he died. I wish I knew.

Ray Huebner moved to Bushton with his twin brother Jay when their parents died in March of 1956. He and Jay were athletes and quickly fit into our class and the town of Bushton. He retired from the Marine Corps in 1982 with the rank of Lieutenant Colonel and died in 2019.

Sam and Ruby Huebner, the parents of Ray and Jay and of their brother Gerald, were on their way to Glen Elder, Kansas, when all three died in a two-car automobile crash a few miles east of Bushton. Sam was the Superintendent of Schools in Glen Elder and Ruby taught math and English. The twin boys finished the school year in Glen Elder but the following year they moved to Bushton to live with Adrian and Ruth Heubner and their sons Ron ('58) and Dennis ('64). The Bushton Huebners encouraged the twins to feel that their "home" throughout their college days at K-State was in Bushton with them.

Jeanne (Volkland) Huebner ('58), Jay's wife, said they made many trips from their home in Jacksonville, Florida, to see Ray before he died. Her husband Jay, she said, never wanted to retire. He simply wants to do more research, as he has done all his adult life as a college professor, and get more patents in his name.

We were glad to have Ray and Jay in our class where they fit in perfectly (Jay was elected President of my Senior Class) and, by the way, helped us out athletically as well. It was a terrible time for them and those of us who knew them are glad they could become a part of our small community. I hope we were a help to them as they must have struggled emotionally for some time although they never let us know if or when they were having a difficult time.

It's hard to believe those three are gone. Phil and Gary

had been gone when our class had its 60-year anniversary celebration at Mildred (Peterson) Dundas' home in Hutchinson, Kansas, in 2017. Ray and Jay were both there with their wives and that's the last time I saw Ray.

There was another youngster who would have been in either the class of '56 or '57 but who died long before we became high school seniors. Charlie Ray was a small boy, quiet and, as I recall, well-liked. He died in a vehicle accident out on the Kansas prairie somewhere. I won't forget him and wish he had lived to finish high school with the rest of us.

Many Bushton High grads served in the military but, among those who served relatively recently, Ray Huebner joined two others who were high ranking officers. They were David Weihe (class of '54), who retired from the Air Force in 1981 as a Colonel, and Don "Hoot" Hiltbrunner who retired from the Marines in 1991 as a Colonel.

Russell Vail, who attended school in Bushton for several years but ultimately graduated from Plains High School in '59, told me about a Bushton farm boy who rose to a three-star Lieutenant General and distinguished himself as commander of the "Big Red One" in World War I and later led the Normandy invasion at Omaha Beach in 1944.

General Clarence Ralph Huebner (1888-1972), also led the First Infantry Division which was the first American military group to meet up with the Russians after Normandy. Russell says General Huebner's story parallels the U.S. Army in the 20th Century. He disdained publicity, Vail says, and therefore his story is seldom told and is not well known.

"All in all," Dale Nordstrom said, "the adults in Bushton set a good example. They were hardworking, honest and, for the most part, kind. I wasn't aware of people in Bushton going to bed hungry. They looked out for one another." He said the time he lived there – from 1937 to 1955 – was a different time. It was a good time to grow up.

Chapter 12

Religion is Booming

Down a country road lies...

EVERYTHING ELSE WAS BOOMING in the fifties. Why not religion, too?

There are those who contend that many of the trends of the fifties – soaring birth rates, economic good times and the focus on normalcy and family – converged to create the religious boom of the decade. Among them is Robert Ellwood, who was a professor in the School of Religion at the University of Southern California in 1997 when Rutgers University Press published his book *The Fifties Spiritual Marketplace: American Religion in a Decade of Conflict.*

Ellwood notes that, in the fifties, churches and schools were being greatly expanded to accommodate the growing population and organized religion was in its heyday. On a typical Sunday morning from 1955 to 1958 almost half of all Americans were attending church. This was the highest percentage in U.S. history. During the 1950s nationwide church membership grew at a faster rate than the population, from 57 percent of the U.S. population in 1950 to 63.3 percent in 1960.

The website https://prezi.com reports that, in the fifties, there were approximately 25 million Catholics in the U.S., 5 million Jews and 8 million Protestants.

Religion flourished in the fifties for several reasons. It was partly because of the ever-expanding spiritual marketplace. Before the war, organized religion was much more restricted, but in the fifties there were a lot of different options available that would appeal to different kinds of people.

Historians say the '50s were the last decade of religious modernism, while the '60s saw the beginning of a postmodern period. It was a time when religion was powerful in American life – partly because most people believed they needed it and there was seemingly nothing to discredit it. It was also because the varied spiritual marketplace proved dynamic and competitive enough to keep it going. It was an age of affluence – sometimes a spendthrift age – in things of the spirit as well as of this world.

In Bushton, Kansas, many of us went to church because it was simply the thing we did whether Catholic or Protestant. Others of us felt called to attend church and to strive for a life that was like that spelled out in the Bible. For me and many of my friends, Christianity was the default religion. If we were in town and were healthy we went to church, sometimes even when we weren't necessarily healthy.

Bushton's First Methodist Church

In my case, Bushton's First Methodist Church (this was before it became the "United" Methodist Church) beckoned from its imposing corner site, with its many concrete steps leading to the immaculate front doors which opened on to a sanctuary which inspired deeply religious thoughts thanks to beautiful stained glass windows, a large choir loft and the majestic pulpit at the center of it all.

The combined Bushton Methodist Church choirs in the mid-'50s. Ally's dad Vernon is standing second from left next to the minister. Choir Director Louise Habiger is partially hidden behind Vernon. Ally's mother Leola is seated at the organ on the right. Ally is three to the right of her father and Wayne is on the front row, third from the right. My sister Linda is standing right behind Wayne. No telling where I was (I may have ducked down in the empty spot in the center of the top row…). This includes a remarkable number of people from a church in such a small town. Note the beautiful stained glass window. There was another just as beautiful on the north wall, to the left.

The church sat at an angle on the corner a block off Main Street and faced southwest. I'm sure some people thought the fact that it did not point in one of the four specific directions was illustrative of a lack of direction from its religious leaders. In fact, I felt guided and directed by Sunday school lessons that explained the Bible in literal terms and in Sunday sermons that illumined the one true path to Christian salvation.

Church and Christianity was a cornerstone of life for many in my family. Ally recently showed me a copy she had run across of what my uncle Willis Koonce, the father of Carol and the man for whom I worked one summer in Chandler, Oklahoma, called his "testimony." In it, he explained about personal encounters he had experienced with Jesus Christ and how important they had been to him and how he hoped for the same kind of experience for the rest of us. Until then, sadly I hadn't realized how devoted a Christian he had become.

Music was a major part of any Sunday service at our Bushton church. Several choirs, populated by various age groups, performed regularly. The adult choir (of which I eventually became a member) sang lustily under the direction of Louise Habiger while Leola Groth (Ally's mother) played the organ with skill and taste. Ally's father Vernon was a choir member, too.

Never mind that one choir member (at least one) every Sunday sat on the front row of the choir loft and very visibly slept through the sermon, or that Harve Hemmer's voice dominated the hymn singing by the congregation, or that we young people usually sat in a group near the front of the sanctuary, probably mainly so we could be near, perhaps next to, a boyfriend or girlfriend.

It's a wonder, thinking back, that Mrs. Habiger allowed me to continue singing in the adult choir after I blurted out a loud "Hallelujah!" during what was supposed to be a silent rest in the "Hallelujah Chorus" one Easter.

Ally and I joined the Lutheran Church in Gunnison after trying to start a Methodist church there but needed more support from the Methodist hierarchy in the area. As Lutherans, though, we especially appreciated Martin Luther's comment that "next to the Word of God, the noble art of music is the greatest treasure in the world."

Ally often remarks about church in Bushton and its importance to her family. She says her Sunday school teachers had great influence on her life and especially credits Leone Henry.

Speaking for the two of us, Ally says "this small town and its values contributed mightily to our growing up years in obvious and subtle ways. Church played an important part in our growing relationship and still does."

After our marriage in the church in Bushton our two children were both baptized there and we continued to attend whenever we were visiting her parents on the farm. We have continued to be church members wherever we have lived and

Ally served as pianist for various churches – Methodist, Episcopal, Lutheran, United Church of Christ, non-denominational and others. We learned and grew from attendance at all of them and value the relationships we established among the members.

"Church" is an important part of the memories of Bushton among many of my classmates.

Lanara Luthi recalls that, upon moving to Bushton, "the first thing we did was to have a tour of the Methodist Church." She quickly learned she was too old to become a member of a Sunday school class whose room greatly appealed to her. The room in which her eventual class met "had cute, small wood chairs for us to use. I thought they were nice and was pleased with that class after all," she said. She took part in a choir and sat in the congregation "under the watchful eye of the minister who would glare at the kids who were not being quiet."

Lanara "loved Matilda Volkland" who was "so nice and a great Sunday school and Bible school teacher." She also recalled sitting in front of Leone Henry and "how much vocal expression she used while praying Lord's Prayer."

Likewise, Millie Sanderson "loved singing in the choir on Sunday" and in Wednesday night rehearsals. She said she once saw Fran Habiger, the son of choir director Louise Habiger at a K-State football game and he said he still sang in a choir in his current church in Hutchinson.

Myretta Bell feels that generosity "of money, time and talent was an asset for Bushton."

She said the Salem Methodist Church, located out of town in the countryside, originally had sermons in both English and German and had a small cemetery which still exists and which is labeled with the German word, "Friedhof." She said "as members died and were buried there, the church needed more space. The man who owned the adjoining property, a Catholic, over the years graciously donated extra acreage with no charge to the church."

She also said, "incidentally, there is no charge for burial plots there." She called this "an act of charity."

Despite the flourishing of religion in the fifties, some

believe that religious conflicts were pronounced. They cite Catholic vs. Protestant and liberal vs. evangelical. The early years saw McCarthyism and Korea. The Cold War was so ubiquitous that children fearing a nuclear explosion often did not believe they would grow to adulthood. Reports say Catholic-Protestant relations were strained by bitter altercations on issues such as parochial schools, public funding and birth control.

Maybe so. But I was a Protestant and many of my friends and classmates were Catholic. I don't recall religious conflicts with any of them. That doesn't mean there weren't any, at least among thinking adults. For the youngsters (I can speak only for those my age) whatever conflicts existed were not as important as the events and attitudes that normally constituted the thoughts and concerns of young people.

Mildred Dundas said that while church activities were centered around the Methodist and Catholic faiths, "friendship with one another was not compromised by this."

However, Neil Denton spoke of a feeling he had that was one of being "segregated" by religion. He said he grew up not far from a family of Catholics and, being Protestant, there was very little interaction with that family. Because most of the Catholic children attended a parochial grade school, he said, when they came to Bushton for the higher grades, they were almost strangers to those who had attended Bushton schools.

Things of a religious nature were about to change. A shift away from the high religiosity of the fifties began by the end of the decade. This was amid the double shocks of 1957: the integration of schools in Little Rock and the success of the Soviet satellite Sputnik. As mainstream religious revival waned Billy Graham's evangelical revival was on the rise. The Cold War and Communism were less on people's mind as a new generation with different cars and rock music was coming into a new world – the 1960s."

A character in Arthur Koestler's 1941 Russian novel *Darkness at Noon* offers some interesting thoughts on human ethics. He calls one concept "Christian and humane" and says this declares the individual to be sacrosanct. The other concept, he says, states that a collective aim justifies all means and demands that the individual should in every way be subordinated and sacrificed to the community.

The discussion about whether America should embrace democracy/Christianity or socialism hadn't really begun in the '50s but this kind of thinking offers food for thought for today's conversations.

While I'm thinking about it, the words "under God" in the Pledge of Allegiance and the phrase "In God we trust" on the back of paper money haven't been there as long as most Americans might think. Those references were inserted in the 1950s during the Eisenhower administration, the same decade that the National Prayer Breakfast was launched, according to writer Kevin Kruse. His 2015 book is *One Nation under God.*

During the Nixon Presidency Ally and I attended one of the National Prayer Breakfasts in Washington, D.C.

Kruse's book investigates how the idea of America as a Christian nation was promoted in the 1930s and '40s when industrialists and business lobbies, chafing against the government regulations of the New Deal, recruited and funded conservative clergy to preach faith, freedom and free enterprise. He says this conflation of Christianity and capitalism moved to center stage in the '50s under Eisenhower's watch. According to the conventional narrative, the Soviet Union discovered the bomb and the United States rediscovered God,

Jonathan Raban, author of *Bad Land,* says that under Eisenhower, the phrase "under god" was snipped out of Lincoln's Gettysburg Address and "spatchcocked" into the pledge by an act of congress in 1954.

In May of that year, *Newsweek* magazine reported: "The man who started the drive is the Rev. George M. Docherty, pastor of the New York Avenue Presbyterian Church, where President Eisenhower worships." In a Lincoln day sermon, the Rev. Docherty observed that there was something missing from the pledge which, he remarked, "could just as well be repeated by little Muscovites pledging allegiance to the hammer and sickle."

Chapter 13

Jocks and Jockesses

Down a country road lies…

CALL ME A JOCK. Actually, you could say that nearly all the boys in high school were "jocks." And so were some of the girls.

That's because in such a small school all the young men were asked to participate in order to field teams in whatever sport was in season, football requiring the largest number. Some of the women students also loved athletics and participated in whatever way was possible. This was prior to Title IX and regulations requiring women's sports.

"I always appreciated the opportunity to grow up in a small town for the variety of sports activities in which average athletes were encouraged to participate," said Darrol Timmons.

Sports were important – to the school district, to the students and to much of the town's population. It's where you went when there was a home game, no matter what the sport. Being able to boast that "we" had beaten Holyrood or Norwich or Sylvia or Geneseo or Lorraine was a source of pride among, not only the athletes, but many of the townspeople as well.

But especially in football.

During my high school years we did very well in football, pretty well in baseball and fairly well in basketball. I wasn't much of a track and field athlete but I remember some very fast students who excelled in the shorter races – Russell Vail and Eugene Hoelscher, for example – and in the longer events – like David Weihe.

1956 basketball ("B" team?)

The '55 football team

The starting Six in '56 – note no facemasks

UNDEFEATED — Coach Calvin Winter huddles with his starting six at Bushton. The team has won four games this season, extending Bushton's winning streak to 21. Left to right are Coach Winter, Ray Huebner, Lyle Komarek, Johnny Heinz, Jack Dohrman, Phillip Henry and Larry Meredith.

Speck Speculates Oct 1956

Bushton Has 21-Game Win Skein; Sixball Is Picking Up New Fans

It began in elementary school, especially in the upper grades – 6 through 8. Basketball was a big deal. In fact, the nearby town of Chase held a basketball tournament every year called the Midget Tournament. Only boys who weighed less than

100 pounds could participate. I recall that the one year I participated in that tournament I barely made the weight limit. Some of us were told by our coach Lawrence Timmons to go the bathroom prior to the weigh-in to help us weigh less than 100 pounds.

We also played baseball in elementary school and, because we had no school buses in those days, we were hauled to away games in the back of a farmer's truck – dozens of young students (boys and girls) crammed together singing, all the way there and back (win or lose) "Ninety-nine Bottles of Beer on the all, ninety-nine bottles of beer. Take one down and pass it around, ninety-eight bottles of beer on the wall." And so on to zero and, if there was time, we started over!

Fran Habiger recalls one such trip when the farm truck in which the group was riding, had to stop for a funeral procession. Mr. Timmons told the students to stand quietly and take off their caps. It's interesting what we remember.

Sue Dahlsten was a high school cheerleader, like my sister Linda. Sue also remembers that there were no school buses. "So, many times I drove a carload of cheerleaders to an away game or rode with another cheerleader," she said.

With all the current safety requirements – local, state and federal – I don't think any school could get away with that kind of transportation these days.

Later, in high school, still without school buses, teams were driven to away games by coaches and parents. Dad was always counted on to drive. It was taken for granted that he would. As I think back, Dad was taken for granted far too often. Like many other parents, I'm sure. I know I took advantage of Dad much too often. But he was always willing to be involved in anything and in any way that I asked. J. D. Vance, in his 1916 book *Hillbilly Elegy*, opines that being able to 'take advantage' of someone is the measure…of having a parent.

We didn't have baseball uniforms in elementary school but that didn't matter because we loved playing baseball. We did have "classy" black uniforms for basketball. In both elementary and high school we were the Bushton Trojans and our colors were black and orange. Cool.

Millie Sanderson says the "Trojan Head" that once adorned one of the entrances to the newest addition to the high school is now in the Bushton Museum (in what was once the drug store).

Sports, in high school, to me at least, were second only to Ally in importance. I loved being an athlete and, win or lose, just being a part of a team in any of the sports was the main thing. I recall that I didn't much like losing but when it happened it didn't take long to forget about getting beat and to begin looking forward to the next game.

During my high school years our football teams were unbeaten in 24 straight games. During my senior year the team from Alden tied us 22-22. But we didn't consider that a loss and the yearbook said "coach Calvin Winter's...Trojans extended their undefeated streak to three seasons and 24 games. During the past six years Bushton has won 41 lost 4 and tied 1."

We played six-man football in those days. Wayne Groth says he was "introduced to six-man football as a freshman and then moved on to eight-man as a sophomore and finally 11-man as a junior and senior." He said he never understood why the changes were made "because we seemed to have smaller class sizes as we got older. But through organized sports we all got to test our talents in athletics."

During the fifties sports nationwide were growing in interest, especially as more and more people purchased television sets. The website https://www.retrowaste.com reports that baseball and boxing were huge in the early part of the decade, while interest in football and golf was growing. As I've reported earlier, the Yankees dominated the decade, but there was great interest in the Cleveland Browns as well. Rocky Marciano and Floyd Patterson were the boxing superstars of the day.

In those days college football was more popular than pro football. For example, the Rose Bowl game between Ohio State and Oregon attracted 98,202 fans. Pro football really started becoming a huge success when it began showing up more and more regularly on television screens.

Athletes like Mickey Mantle, Hank Aaron and Jim Brown were household names. Finally, baseball was completely integrated as dozens of African American ballplayers filled major league lineups. Rocky Marciano enjoyed a historic, undefeated run as a boxer between 1952 and 1956. Hockey was becoming more popular as well.

Ohio was stamped the center of the football world when Ohio State was crowned national champions by the AP following an unbeaten season. Alan Ameche, Wisconsin's bruising runner, was the college standout player of the year, winning several awards.

In 1954, Football-related deaths saddened us all, with 19 deaths being charged to the sport — 12 in high school, 2 in college, 2 in pro or semi-pro and 3 in sand-lot play.

Skip ahead to 1957, my senior year, when I was more aware of sports on a national level than ever before.

That year, to my delight, Milwaukee beat the Yankees in the World Series. But also that year, the New York Giants announced that in 1958 they would move to San Francisco, and the Brooklyn Dodgers said they would leave Flatbush for Los Angeles. After years and years of the, more or less, status quo in pro baseball the sports world seemed to me to be fracturing. Still, Major league attendance was up almost 3% for the year, with 10 of the 16 clubs showing increases. The American League drew almost 8.2 million. The National League 8.8 million.

These facts may not seem important to many readers but to a high school senior who loved sports, the news was of great magnitude.

Another thing: both 1957 pennant races were decided on Monday, September 23, six days before the end of the season. This is of vital importance to Denny Meredith-Orr, our son-in-law who grew up in Quincy, Illinois, and is a lifelong die-hard fan of the St. Louis Cardinals.

In 1957 the Braves and the Cardinals had the biggest battle for the flag. It was an 11th-inning home run by Hank Aaron against the Cardinals that clinched the pennant for Milwaukee.

College basketball was important to Kansans that year because Wilt Chamberlain led the University of Kansas to the national title game in the NCAA tournament. I saw Chamberlain play against K-State and again that season in the game in

Lawrence when I was a freshman.

Unfortunately for KU, North Carolina won the 1957 championship game in triple overtime 54-53 and finished a perfect 32 and 0.

One more thing about college football that year, but only because it involved the University of Oklahoma which I had once hoped to attend. I still follow and root for the Sooners.

The most stunning upset of the 1957 college football season was engineered by Notre Dame, which won six of nine games after a 2-8 season the year before. The Fighting Irish shocked Oklahoma, 7-0, in Norman, to halt the Sooners' 47-game winning streak. Ironically, Oklahoma's streak had started one week after a Notre Dame loss in 1953. Oklahoma finished the season ranked #4.

Meanwhile, back in Bushton –

I must tell you (in case you don't already know) about the athletic ability of Russell Vail. As mentioned earlier, he graduated from Plains High School in 1959. I wish he could have stayed in Bushton.

Russell Vail wins another race

He was a track star. While at Southwestern College he was a three-time all-American and held 16 school records. His list of awards and accomplishments is too long to list here but suffice it to say he holds one national record, three individual national championships, six individual Michigan State Records and dozens of individual state championships. He says, however, that his mother, Ruth Elizabeth, was a greater athlete than he. She set the National High School Girls Scoring Record in 1929 of 90 points but, in that game, played only a few seconds of the final quarter. She also scored 40 to 60 points in multiple games and was picked to play in the National Tournament in Wichita which today is the equivalent of making the National All-Star Team (or maybe the Olympic team).

My wife Ally says she never saw the second half of any football game in which I played because she spent the time changing from her band uniform and getting ready for the dance that would follow the game in the VFW Hall across town.

Bushton High School had a marching band that performed at halftime of every home football game. There was also a pep band that played at basketball games. Ally played the flute.

Lanara Luthi said the games were important "but I think even more important were the sock hops after the home games. The dances were popular," she said, "but it was hard to participate when the boys stayed on one side of the room and girls on the other." She said Ladies Choice helped mix it up some. "The girls were much braver."

Ally and I never had a problem about having a dance partner.

Ally and me at one of the after-game dances in 1956

Still dancing and hugging. Photos are '57, '58, '61 and 2011.

Several Bushton graduates had other recollections of our home football games.

Fran Habiger, for example, said he remembers "a small group of bleachers on the east side of the field while the rest of the field was surrounded by cars for each game." People stayed in their cars and honked their horns each time Bushton scored a touchdown. "It was LOUD!" he said. He also recalled that once the lights went out during a game and "all the cars turned their lights on and we were able to finish the game by car lights."

Here's what I recall about six-man football.

We played with a three-man offensive line—two ends and a center – with two backs and a quarterback (me) in the backfield. On defense, we sometimes played a two-man defensive front and sometimes a three-man front.

On offense, everyone was an eligible pass receiver, even the center. But the quarterback could not personally advance the ball across the line of scrimmage. The ball had, first, to be handed off to a running back or it could be passed to a receiver downfield. And, in the backfield, the football had to be delivered to a running back with a clear pass. It was illegal to stuff the ball into a back's stomach without a clear pass with the ball in the air.

In addition, the field was 40 yards wide by 80 yards long, as opposed to the 50X100-yard size field in 11-man football. Also, in the six-man game, a team must advance the ball 15 yards for a first down rather than ten.

My favorite plays included the 12-fake-35 where I would fake handing the ball to the fullback who charged the line, toss it to a halfback running around the end and then block for the running back. The 12-fake-35-pass was the same except I faked the ball to both the fullback and halfback and then passed it downfield to a receiver.

We also had a running play which went one direction or the other, depending on whether the defense was lined up in a two- or three-man set. I once called a "strong to the right 15" play which meant that we lined up for a run to the right but if the defense was in a two-man alignment we were to run to the left. I ran the wrong way and found myself alone with the ball and unable to advance it past the line of scrimmage. I got clobbered by a defensive lineman and had the breath knocked out of me. That's as close as I ever came to being hurt and my teammates let me know I had screwed up.

We had many other plays but those linger most in my mind.

With so few players on the field it was easy to see when a mistake was made, and who made it. It was a wide open game with players and footballs flying around for all to see.

I got to play a great deal as a high school junior. In one game I remember punting the ball which hit Neil Denton in the back of his helmet when he was blocking for me. Neil thinks that maybe he was punting and the ball hit me. Whatever.

I also recall one game in which Neil, a running back, got loose on a long touchdown run. His dad, Bill Denton (a rather portly man) got so excited he ran down the sideline step-by-step with Neil. I didn't know either of them could run that fast.

At the end of our senior year our yearbook reported that Phil Henry led the scoring with 106 points. "Other scorers," the book reported, "included John Heinz 63, Eugene Hoelscher 30, and Ray Huebner 30." Others who scored included LaVerne Renville, Doug Volkland, Jack Dohrman, Darrol Timmons, and Lyle Komarek. "Larry Meredith fired 11 touchdown passes," the yearbook said.

In basketball that year, we won 10 games and lost 8. Not a bad year and it surely was fun.

In baseball, the yearbook doesn't list wins and losses but says Bushton was Champion of the Quivira League that year. I was a pitcher.

It is interesting to see team photos from several sports in the yearbooks. Pretty much the same guys appear in each photo, just wearing a different uniform.

We played basketball in a "new" gym. The old gymnasium, which I played in during my elementary school years, was very small. In fact, it was so small that the center circle overlapped the two freethrow circles at either end of the basketball floor. I'm sure visiting teams that had larger, regular-sized, gyms found their stamina was better in our small gym.

JaLayne Clark remembers that the gym had a stage at one end and "only had room on the sides for one row of folding chairs." It also had a balcony with just two rows of seats, she said.

In 1954, when I was a high school freshman, a bid of a little more than $210,000 was accepted for a new addition to the school building. For the high school it would include a modern science room, an "ultra-modern" auditorium and gymnasium, modern shop facilities and shop classroom, an additional classroom, new offices, lavatories, storeroom and workroom.

The bid also included a remodeled and added-on elementary section. It would provide two additional classrooms, an office, storage accommodations, additional lavatories, a teacher's workroom, and enhancements for kindergarteners and the old gym.

To me, the most important was the "ultra-modern" high school gymnasium and auditorium. We would be able to play basketball in a regular-sized gym with adequate seating for the crowds we expected and which ultimately almost filled the bleachers.

"Girls' sports competition hardly existed" said Lanara Luthi. She said sixth, seventh and eighth grade girls did get to play an occasional softball game when the boys had a scheduled baseball game. "The girls would also play volleyball before the boys' basketball games once in a while." She said. They would also compete in a track meet yearly at a Geneseo Play Day. "We had spent some recess time jumping and running to ready us for the meet. The high jump and pole vault pit landing areas were simply sand. It is a good thing we didn't jump very high or our tail bones would suffer."

She said she lived in a house next to an alfalfa field on the edge of town. "We spent hours hitting baseballs out into the field for the neighborhood boys. "That was after we got to know them better," she said. "Up until then we spent time throwing dirt clods at each other from across the street."

Three more stories from Fran Habiger –

Fran recalled one year when a football game was scheduled the night after Halloween. Coach Winter told team members to be home by 10:00 p.m. Telling themselves that the coach would never know, Fran and other team members stayed out much later "dragging Main. "The next Monday I was running laps along with others because I was not home at 10:00 p.m.," Fran said. "How did Coach Winter know that?" Fran said the Coach and his wife Marie lived on Main Street and he knew every car that team members or their parents drove. "He sat on his porch in the dark and caught every one of us," he said. "Only in a small town would the coach recognize every car his football players drove."

On another Halloween night Fran and other football players decided to go to the football field and take the tackling dummy to coach Winter's front porch. "As we were taking it down," he said, "Mr. Komarek, the city policeman, showed up." Instead of getting after the boys, Fran said, "when we told him what we wanted to do, he helped us. Only in a small town."

And finally, Fran said when the VFW opened up their building for dances after home games "we always had to check the refrigerator in the kitchen of the building to see how much liquor was in there." To Fran's knowledge, "no one ever touched it."

So, I was a jock. But that term was applied to almost every boy in the school. Still, it was important and we all learned something valuable when we played on a team. I have to give our coach, Calvin Winter, the credit for that. Thanks Coach.

Chapter 14

The Wind Comes Sweeping Down the Plain

Down a country road lies the…

ONE CAN'T HONESTLY TALK much about Kansas in the '50s without bringing up the weather.
　Here we go.
　In the summer it was scorching hot and in the winter it was freezing cold.
　That's what I remember.
　However, Ally and I lived in Gunnison, Colorado, for nearly 20 years while I was with Western Colorado University and she was teaching elementary music and then was on the WCU music faculty. Gunnison is known as one of the coldest cities in the country but I don't think I was ever as cold there as I had been in many Bushton, Kansas, winters.
　The humidity in Gunnison was very low and we didn't have much wind. In Kansas it was just the opposite. Maybe that's why it seemed colder in Kansas.
　I have often (only half- jokingly) said until we moved to Colorado I never knew snow fell straight down. I thought it always came horizontally, like in a Kansas blizzard.
　Speaking of Kansas blizzards –
Once, when driving Ally home from a date, we were caught in a sudden blizzard and the car (it might have been the Pontiac) slid off into the ditch. Repeated efforts failed to get us unstuck. Fortunately, we were only about a mile and a half from the farm so we bundled up as best we could and walked. Terribly embarrassed, I told her father what had happened.
　As I recall, without a word he donned heavy winter

clothing, led me out to the barn, started up a large tractor, drove us (exposed to the weather) to the stranded car, hooked up to it and pulled it out. I thanked him and drove home – very slowly. He never said a word about the incident to me, for which I have been eternally grateful. Actually, I think he was amused.

Ally's brother Wayne told me his family was often "snowed in" at the farm "and that meant a break from going to school and waiting for the road grader to come by and clear the roads." Other farm kids had similar recollections.

Wayne recalled one winter when the roads were impassable around Thanksgiving because of a heavy snow. "Somehow," he said, "a couple of men who worked on the oil wells ended up at our house and lived with us for a couple of days until the roads were clear. That was an unusual Thanksgiving."

Wayne also had the experience of sliding into a ditch. "I was several miles from home," he said, "so I went to the nearest neighbor, Ed Habiger" (father of Fran and Sue). Habiger fired up his tractor in the freezing weather and pulled Wayne's car out of the ditch. "That's the sign of the strong sense of community and neighbors helping neighbors," Wayne said.

I've already mentioned the time Myretta Bell got stuck on a muddy road and was rescued by Marvin Weihe.

I suspect the same thing happened to many of my classmates but it wasn't necessarily a topic of conversation. It was simply what friends did for friends.

Or what the father of a girlfriend did for the boyfriend.

Thank God.

But, back to "typical" Kansas weather –

The website weather.gov lists what it terms "the Top Ten Weather Events of the 20th Century for central, south central, and southeast Kansas." Among them were tornadoes in 1917, 1927, 1955, 1958, 1990 and 1991.

The site also lists an "honorable mention" of two tornadoes which touched down and affected portions of central and south central Kansas on November 10, 1915. The first moved across Barton County, just west of Bushton, and hit the southeastern sections of Great Bend, causing one million dollars in damage" (a great deal more money in 21st Century dollars). The website says "160 homes were destroyed and at least 1,000 sheep were killed on nearby ranches." Debris from Great Bend was carried 85 miles and hundreds of dead ducks fell from the sky 25 miles northeast of the end of the tornado path which was just west of Claflin (fewer than a dozen miles west of Bushton). On the same day another tornado moved across portions of Sumner and Sedgwick counties in southern Kansas.

That is illustrative of what can happen in a Kansas tornado.

Other tornadoes have devastated various parts of Kansas (although, to my knowledge, Bushton itself was never hit). In May of 1927, for example, a tornado in Kingman, Reno and McPherson Counties (McPherson is barely 30 miles east of Bushton) killed 10 people and injured 300. The tornado was said to range from one-half to two miles wide and was on the ground for nearly 100 miles.

And, believe it or not, there was a major flood in Kansas (normally a very dry state) in 1998 when nearly a foot of rain fell over parts of south central and southeast Kansas resulting in flooding of many rivers. The Arkansas, Cottonwood, Whitewater and Walnut Rivers recorded all-time record levels. This became known as the "Halloween Flood" and resulted in 37.8 million dollars in damage and the evacuation of 5,300 people. One person died in the flood and two were injured.

Of course, no discussion of Kansas weather would be complete without mentioning the Dust Bowl of the 1930s. The Dust Bowl ranks among the most significant weather events of the century and literally changed the face of the Great Plains. Fortunately, Bushton was on the eastern edge of the Dust Bowl and Ally's father says they were affected very little by it. Still, the all-time record high temperature of 114 degrees was set on August 12, 1936, in Wichita in southern Kansas. That was the year of Ally's parent's wedding. That time frame also produced the longest stretch of 100 degree days of 20.

Finally, the two extremes of weather are illustrated by the blizzard of 1971 and the sizzling summer of 1980.

Kansas is well-known for its violent spring weather which

often produces deadly tornadoes. But winter can also spawn dangerous weather. On February 21, 1971, an intense winter storm buried southern Kansas under ten to 13 inches of snow. The storm packed such a terrific punch that north-northeast winds gusting up to 40 mph produced near zero visibility, bringing a large portion of southern Kansas to a standstill.

Conversely, blistering heat arrived in June of 1980 when the mercury soared to 103 degrees. Afternoon high temperatures broke the 100-degree barrier every day for the rest of the month, culminating in a monthly high of 110 degrees on June 30. But the heatwave wasn't over. In July, temperatures cleared 100 degrees on 24 out of 31 days, including an eighteen-day stretch. At the same time, Wichita for example, received only 1.8 inches of rain during June and July, and less than half an inch of that fell in July.

Richard Rhodes includes a wonderful sentence about weather in his 1989 book *Farm: A Year in the Life of an American Farmer*. He writes of clouds: "wispy cirrus playing the aristocrat, a demagogic thunderhead moving against a parliament of mackerel sky."

I don't think we ever had many consecutive days of temps higher than 100 in Bushton in the summers of the fifties, but it often seemed like we did. Those of us working in the farm fields always carried jugs of water and we sweltered on other outdoor jobs. Phil Henry and I sweated massively the summer we cleaned and organized the attic of Bushton's mercantile store. And all for a watermelon apiece!

I also don't think we ever had to play a football game in a snowstorm, although I recall one during a rainstorm in which we barely scored enough points to win before a sparse crowd. I don't even recall who we were playing against.

But, weather in Kansas? As they say, "if you don't like it, wait a minute."

Whoever "they" are.

Chapter 15

Time to "Light Out"

Down a country road...

LIKE MARK TWAIN'S Huckleberry Finn, many of us felt we had to "light out" upon graduation from high school or college and, though we called Bushton our "home town" or even "home," most of us who did "light out" would never live there again. At the end of Twain's book Huck says "I reckon I got to light out for the Territory ahead of the rest, because Aunt Sally she's going to adopt me and sivilize me, and I can't stand it. I been there before." *The Adventures of Huckleberry Finn* was first published in the United Kingdom in December of 1884 and in the U.S. in February of 1885, two years before Bushton was founded.

Because the word "Territory" is capitalized it can be assumed that Huck was referring to Indian Territory (now the state of Oklahoma). It is also easy to imagine that he made it to that now-famous part of the country and that, assuming he did, he (fictionally) took part in the Oklahoma Land Rush of 1889 with a few others (an estimated 50,000 people who were vying for their piece of the available two million acres). In southern Kansas and surrounding the "Territory," thousands of people on horseback, in buggies and covered wagons, and even afoot, were gathered in camps on April 22 of 1889 waiting for the gunshot that would signal the start of the frantic race for free land. Even the Santa Fe Railway was prepared to take any number of people from its station at Arkansas City, Kansas, and deposit them in almost any part of Oklahoma as soon as the law allowed.

The resulting land rush has gone down in history as one of the most noteworthy events of Western Civilization.

Like many others (though *un*like Huck Finn) I hadn't "been there," wherever "there" was. Nevertheless, I felt the need to "light out."

After Ally and I were married in 1961 we did "light out" and began our journey from Bushton into a fascinating but largely unknown world that beckoned us like Odysseus was beckoned to leave Ithaca to participate in the Trojan War.

Even though we didn't know where we would eventually land after we "lit out" it was exciting to speculate about our future and to wonder where we would settle, raise our children and build our future lives.

Though we were not off to a war or to the excruciating or violent adventures that awaited Odysseus, we left our "ruralness" behind and moved to the "large city" of Wichita, Kansas.

There were some who graduated with me, or within a year or more before or after me, who were anxious to leave Bushton and the rural life. I was not one of them. I felt it necessary that I attend college and I had to leave Bushton to do that. Later, Ally and I knew our lives were destined to be in locales far from the village of our youth. But I can't say I was eager to go.

Heroes are defined as "individuals who go out into the world and come home changed, seeing the world in a fresh way, bearing the wisdom of their experience as news." That news, some believe, "serves the stay-at-homes in their efforts toward making sense of themselves and of what they are attempting to make of their lives."

Ally and I did, indeed, venture out into the world, and although we no doubt changed, I suspect we didn't bring home much of that experience. I guess you could say we never did come home except to visit.

These days, we learn, people are "staying home," meaning they are staying where they know how to live and what to care about. Some believe that there is not much value any more to the idea that going away to seek your fortune is the right road toward anything that matters.

Many of my classmates also found it necessary to "light out" and addresses on the alumni class list that Dennis Huebner ('64) maintains for us include the following states (in no particular order): Kansas, Florida, Texas, Oklahoma, Missouri, Oregon, New Mexico, Indiana, Minnesota, North Carolina, Arkansas, Alabama, Montana, Washington, Virginia, Georgia, Nevada, Illinois, New Hampshire, California, South Dakota, Wyoming, Louisiana, Ohio, Nebraska, Colorado, Connecticut, Iowa and South Carolina. There are probably some I missed.

Not every Bushton grad feels the need to "light out" and, although most leave town, some don't go very far. Jalayne Clark settled in Lyons, barely 20 miles from Bushton and, like Jalayne, her family hasn't strayed far. Jalayne says she has five sons, 12 grandchildren and 27 great grandchildren ranging in age from 22 months to 22 years. Three of her sons are coaches – one at Barton County Community College (Barton County adjoins Rice County, in which Bushton is located), one at Chase, Kansas, High School and one in Lyons High School. One granddaughter is studying medicine at the University of Kansas and another is a basketball star at Sterling College located just south of Lyons.

One of Jalayne's daughters-in-law attended Bushton High School and four grandchildren attended school there.

So, not everyone "lights out" for the Territory and, among those who do, many do not go far away.

But, to find the kind of life we dreamed of, Ally and I had to leave Bushton.

In the fall of 1963 Hallmark Cards in Kansas City, Mo, brought us to a hotel near the J.C. Nichols Plaza in preparation for my interview for a position in the Advertising and Sales Promotion Division (a job I ultimately got and stayed in for two years). We had been living in a city of roughly 300,000 people, but Kansas City was much larger and a whole new ballgame for us. While I felt we were game for living in a large city, I had some early trepidation about how we would deal with it. The Interstate highway system was still mostly a dream in those days and I would have to drive to work from the Kansas side (Overland Park) on regular city streets and go to work with thousands of other employees. I would share an office with another person and peer through glass walls, past two other offices, right into the eyes of a Vice President who had responsibility for advertising, public relations and sales promotion. Could I handle it? And how would we adjust to city living?

I shouldn't have worried. I dealt with it well enough.

Looking from my office at Hallmark Cards through two other offices to the Vice President's. Big Brother was watching!

As she has proven throughout our married life, Ally showed her mettle and illustrated her toughness and willingness to handle whatever life dealt her in a wonderful manner. In fact, she also landed a job at Hallmark. After two years, and the birth of our daughter Suzy, I decided Hallmark was too big a firm for me and we moved back to Wichita where I joined Friends University, a small Quaker-related private college, and began my life in academia. In Wichita I also began my life as the father of a son when Greg was born to us in 1967.

Ally, armed with a teaching degree, took a job teaching elementary school music in the suburban schools of Pleasant Valley and we were happy.

We would eventually spend 31 years in the town of Emporia, Kansas, (population around 35,000) where I was on the staff and faculty of Emporia State University and ran my own video production company, Innovative Communications Corporation. We would then spend 20 years in Gunnison, Colorado (population 7,000) while I was with Western Colorado University before settling (for good, we hope) in a rural area in the central Rockies just outside Redstone, Colorado, not far from

Aspen and within a few miles of our children and grandchildren.

But we never forgot our roots in Bushton, Kansas, situated in flat prairie farmland almost exactly in the center of the state and nearly at the geographical center of the United States

182 – **REAL, RURAL**

Chapter 16

And, in Conclusion...

Down a country road lies the direction for a life.

THE 1950S WERE THE PERFECT time to grow up rural. Looking back, however, I have come to believe that any time is a good time to grow up rural. However, in the 1950s, whether we realized it or not, the world was rapidly changing and those of us around my age were not only helping effectuate that change, but we were changing right along with the rest of the world. We were growing, of course, and maturing, but we were also forming attitudes; we were deciding what was important and what was not worth our time, effort or mental energy. And just like young people everywhere – in the small towns and on the farms, in the cities and the steel plants and on the crowded streets – young people were beginning to think about living in a world that was different from that in which they had grown up and wondering how they might help make that world better for everyone in it.

A character in Arthur Koestler's Russian novel *Darkness at Noon* speaks of working in "the amorphous raw material of history itself."

In the '50s history seemed to simply "happen." The world surged one way and then another in a formless and fluid manner. One day we were looking forward to owning our first television set, listening to this wild southerner named Elvis and not worrying about much except an upcoming History test only to wake up the next morning and find that a small satellite was orbiting the earth and the U.S. had nothing to do with it. The young men of my age had just about decided that, because WWII had been successfully completed, military service would not be necessary for us. Suddenly, however, South Korea was invaded by North Koreans and we began to wonder which branch of military service we might most logically fit into and how we would look in which uniform – and wondering if we would experience cowardice in the face of battle.

Young women were reading about something called "the pill" and hoping it was true, that perhaps they were to have more control over their bodies than they had ever dreamed.

Civil rights became an issue and we had to scramble to figure out just what that meant. Few of us had ever had any contact with black people but suddenly some of us would be so empathetic to their plight that the only answer to our concern seemed to be to catch the next bus to Selma or Montgomery and then figure out what to do next.

Joe McCarthy's pronouncement that hundreds of Communists existed in our own government sent shock waves throughout the U.S. and reached deep into rural America where few understood how anything but the kind of America most of us knew and loved could ever be even considered, much less attempted.

Many of the changes that were occurring in the world would not become easily apparent until many of us reached adulthood or at least the beginning of it. In those days most of us trusted our elected officials to do the right thing and to make decisions for the good of the people they represented. There were some, though, who so distrusted anyone with power over them that they planned for an Armageddon that would send us all into oblivion. The specter of nuclear annihilation hovered overhead like a giant umbrella and many feared it was inevitable that nuclear bombs would soon rain down on all of us.

Still, most of us felt that despite the horrific fears that caused many sleepless nights all would be well. There were too many reasons for things not to go right. Each of us would grow up strong and straight and smart. We would have a beautiful wife or a handsome husband and our children would be attractive and brilliant and talented.

And I'm sure that's exactly the way it has turned out.

But probably not for everyone.

Some of us had to go to Vietnam and some did not return from that convoluted war.

Some of us made poor decisions and have led a life far different from what had been envisioned.

Others of us were the lucky ones. The lives we have led, the families we have been fortunate to raise, the careers we have enjoyed and the travelling we have done has combined to make our lives fun, interesting and worthwhile.

I grieve for those who have not been as fortunate.

In the foreword to Koestler's *Darkness at Noon* Peter Viereck writes: "The truth of beauty does not consist in a theoretical description or explanation of things; it consists, rather, in the 'sympathetic vision' of things."

I admit that my description of my growing up years in Bushton, Kansas, arises from a sympathetic vision that no doubt excludes many memories of the negative aspects of my life. I make no apologies for that. This book was written in part as a way to expunge the harsh realities of certain memories as well as to, in a way, relive the wonder and absolute enjoyment of living in rural America before we became so divided and biased as a country that potential friendships never came to fruition while some nearly lifelong comradeships were destroyed. The world I grew up in is the world I want my grandchildren to know about. They may not believe it but, as a famous TV newscaster used to say, "that's the way it was."

****

I was about to write *finis* to this manuscript when Ally and I received word that Bob Winter, a close friend of more than 50 years had died. His wife Joyce and all four of their children and grandchildren continue to live in the Topeka, Kansas, area. It was a drive of more than 13 hours one-way but we felt we simply must attend the funeral.

On the drive home we made a detour and drove into the town of Bushton.

I now wish we had not.

Bushton has changed.

Not only has it become significantly smaller, but it has also become, it seems to me, far less useful as a marketplace and supplier of goods for local and area residents.

Some stores have closed, buildings have been razed, and many streets have not been kept free of potholes or debris.

Bushton's Main Street in 2020.

The home I lived in (the "new" house pictured on page 39), and the one Ally's grandmother took such pride in keeping neat and clean, are both dilapidated and worn looking. Each requires paint and simply need to have the appearance that someone who lives there cares about the building. Many other homes in the town seem to suffer from the same lack of care.

The Bushton United Methodist Church, however, looks to me as it always has. The exterior is neat and window frames are painted. We did not go inside. Let's remember it as it was and not risk finding sadness inside.

The school Ally and I attended (pictured on page 70) has changed considerably. The old building is gone and a new one has replaced it. The High School has been "consolidated" with another in a nearby community and Bushton now has only a middle school. The baseball field has disappeared although the football field remains.

On the positive side, the town has converted the former drug store and post office building into a fine historical museum. There is evidence of small industry. A modern convenience store adorns the Main Street and a new "Community Center" sits proudly to the north of the grain elevator near where the VFW building once hosted after-game dances.

Still, I now know I should have taken the advice of author Amor Towles (see page 38) and not returned to view the place I left for good more than 60 years ago.

Libraries and bookstores feature many non-fiction books about the sad state of rural America. They include such titles as *The Left Behind; decline and rage in rural America* (2018); *Worlds Apart: poverty and politics in rural America* (1999); *Consumers in the Country: technology and social change in rural America* (2000); *Children of the Land: adversity and success in rural America* (2000); and *Worlds Apart: why poverty persists in rural America* (1999).

There are many more.

However, mixed signals beam from the farmyards of rural America, at least the part we drove through. Many former beautiful farm homes with wide porches and dormer windows are being destroyed by wind and weather, simply left to rot on sagging foundations while trees and bushes clog once loved lawns. Barns and other outbuildings are uncared for and lean precariously toward the ground.

In other places, often only a few hundred yards from the farmstead just described, stand new homes, often of brick, with new and sturdy outbuildings surrounding them.

Some farmers have simply given up while others are succeeding. Perhaps the younger members of a family chose not to farm but to move to a city. In other cases, perhaps a neighbor farmer who took over from his parents has purchased the failed farmer's land and survives because he now has enough land to make farming profitable. Or perhaps oil has been discovered on his land.

While I was saddened by what I found in my small part of rural America, I understand the reasons for the changes and appreciate the farmers and small town residents who continue to populate the plains and other rural areas of the United States. I am especially encouraged that farms and small towns like Bushton continue to exist.

If even a small majority of those who populate rural

America continue to maintain the values, work ethic and love of country that those of my age witnessed in the middle of the 20th Century we should all rejoice in the belief that there is great hope and opportunity for our country for many decades ahead.

Former Secretary of Agriculture Tom Vilsack once said: *People don't understand rural America. Sixteen percent of our population is rural, but 40 percent of our military is rural. I don't believe that's because of a lack of opportunity in rural America. I believe that's because if you grow up in rural America, you know you can't just keep taking from the land. You've got to give something back.*

To me, that's simply one example of the value of a strong rural background.

* * * *

Ally and I have travelled the world a great deal, sometimes with our children and at other times simply enjoying the company of one another. We have visited much of Europe, Russia and elsewhere. I spent a month in the far reaches of China on a consulting trip during which I never saw a fork and ate strange food that was never identified. On occasion, in many of those foreign nations, I felt more genuinely welcomed than I have frequently felt in parts of the U.S., but I won't risk the ire of some by saying where that was.

Both Millie Sanderson and Myretta Bell spoke of having travelled. Millie said she had always wanted to visit Rome and Greece and she has since been able to realize that dream and I'm sure she has visited other countries as well. Likewise, Myretta has travelled widely. "But," she says, "I'm still a country girl at heart."

The growing up years of my life and, I suspect, the lives of many of my classmates, was governed, in some large part, by the four seasons – fall, winter, spring and summer. For me, the seasons had less to do with changing weather and more to do with which sports uniform I wore. In the fall it was the shoulder pads and helmet of a football uniform; in the winter it was shorts and tennis shoes for basketball; in the spring as the weather warmed we donned hot wool and long stockings for baseball and/or shorts and cleats for track and field. In the heat of summer some of us continued to play baseball in the evenings for one team or another and labored under the sizzling sun during the day at various jobs. But we were young and had the stamina for such a schedule.

Through it all, the "sympathetic vision" I have of life in those days is one of absolute pleasure, of less worry and more wonderment at the world around me, of the joy of being with friends and experimenting with ideas, abilities and even language, and of the excitement and anguish of first (and lasting) love.

Many of my classmates share a similar vision of those days.

First, Ally. Always first, Ally.

"Little did I know," she said, "of the influences Bushton and the surrounding areas would have on my life. Being born into a loving and hard-working farm family with a strong work ethic and stable up-bringing has shaped me to this day."

She also said, bless her heart, "my future husband and love of my life came riding into my life on his bicycle and all these years later we're still happily riding along."

She believes strongly that "the environment of this small town and its values contributed mightily to my growing up years through obvious and subtle ways. The church played an important role in our relationship and it still does."

The rural life was also important to Ally's brother Wayne. "When talking to someone I don't know well," he said, "I'm proud to throw into the conversation that I grew up on a farm in Kansas." He said it is a way of defining his background and experiences as a young person.

And my sister Linda said "I thank God for my childhood years in Bushton and for the many wonderful people there who blessed me with their lives." She said she loved them and she loved "that little country town."

Linda said she didn't dream that "my life there and the world of the '40s and '50s would ever end, or that our lives would change in the many ways they have."

Like many of us, Linda admits that she almost questions if it was real or if it was just a sweet dream.

It was no dream Linda. It was real. But memories of it are softened, I'm sure, by the sympathetic visions that linger within the hearts of many of us.

Some have no sympathetic visions. Their memories are of harsh times and feelings of distrust and a lack of love.

Some, like Gwen Lord harbor certain longings for those days. "As I have gotten older," she said, "the thing I miss the most is the rustling of the green and golden wheat."

Others, like Bonnie Housley, admit they "have absolutely no nostalgia for the rural life or the good old days."

Bonnie, and others, find no reason to be "nostalgic" about growing up rural. They have no sympathetic vision about the '50s and the lives they were forced to live during that time deserve no fond memories. Hopefully, for most of them, like Bonnie, their lives have turned out to be good and full of love and enjoyment.

A contemporary American politician has said "*The American Dream* is a term that is often misunderstood. It isn't really about becoming rich or famous. It is about things much simpler and more fundamental than that." Who said that? I'll leave it to you to pick a politician, political party and ideology. It could have come from anyone.

Most of us survived the '50s intact and have grown into mature, thoughtful adults whose lives have included, in some way, helping make the world a better place for those who are not as fortunate.

Somehow, we all managed to live through spankings, lead paint, rusty playgrounds, second-hand smoke, toy guns, no seatbelts, no helmets, drinking from the hose and other so-called life-threatening acts or omissions.

Much of what we now enjoy and often take for granted was made possible by those first steps taken in the 1950s. Some say it was a "plain and boring" decade, but the inventions, experiments and other forward-moving acts helped mold, not only our country, but us as well, and were important to our development into the persons we have become.

I am glad that I grew up rural and that something (some

call it God's will) took me and my family to Bushton, Kansas, at precisely the right time in my life.

THE END

192 – **REAL, RURAL**

ACKNOWLEDGEMENTS

There are many who deserve thanks and praise for their contributions to this book. I owe special appreciation to those who spoke to me or wrote letters and emails with their thoughts about "growing up rural" or who provided other valuable information. They are, in no special order:

Russell Vail ('59), Fran Habiger ('56), Sue (Habiger) Dahlsten ('58), Darrol Timmons ('58), Marilyn (Behnke) Wilkens ('56), Millie (Heiken) Sanderson ('56), Myretta (Behnke) Bell ('58), Rita (McKay) Hammon ('60), Donnal Hiltbrunner ('56), Jo (Lindsay) Hodges ('57), Jeanne Ann (Volkland) Huebner ('58), Dale Nordstrom ('55), Lanara (Ostrander) Luthi ('58), Bonnie (Gregory) Housley ('58), Linda (Meredith) Byers ('60), Shirley Mullenix ('57), Joy (Long) Nickerson ('55), Dennis Huebner ('64), Jalayne (Wolford) Clark ('56), Gwen (Lindsay) Lord ('58), Wayne Groth ('61), Mildred (Peterson) Dundas ('57), Neil Denton ('56), and Alyce Lyn (Groth) Meredith ('58).

Thanks to Ally, Linda Byers, Suzy Meredith-Orr, Don Hiltbrunner (Hoot), Myretta Bell, Darrol Timmons and Darrell Munsell for reading early drafts of the manuscript and commenting on it, proofreading and making important suggestions. Each one of them helped greatly improve the book's early drafts

REASONS

The reasons I wrote this book (a kind of "Memoir") are many and varied. First of all, I wanted to respond to the many criticisms I hear today of the rural America I know and love. As I grow older and must deal with a country that is so politically divided and so vastly different in other ways from the one in which I grew up, I wanted to put into writing some of what I remember about my early life and try to describe (admittedly with a "sympathetic vision") the kind of world – good and bad – I knew as a youth.

I tried, and know I failed, to adequately express exactly how important Ally has been to me – as a faithful and loving wife, as a young beauty who was so special and meaningful to me as I formed opinions and planned for the future, and now as one who shares a history with me that makes remembering those years even more specific and valuable. Ally also joined me as we began (and continued) a life of church membership and a love of a good and merciful God.

It is also important to me that my children (now adults) and my grandchildren (no longer "children") know something about how it was "back in the day" and maybe even something about why I am the person I have become. Our grandchildren are Colorado natives who have travelled very little outside the mountain west. While they grew up on several wonderful acres with horses and a variety of other animals (all with mountain river frontage) they can't officially be termed "rural." Although we have taken them on trips to such locations as Washington, D.C. and Santa Fe, their exposure to the Kansas prairie (probably annoyingly uninteresting to them) has been limited to brief trips, for example, to attend their grandfather's 100th birthday party and later, for a memorial service in his honor. I hope this book will help make positive sense of the early lives of their great grandparents and their grandparents – Ally and me.

And I hope that our children – Suzy and Greg – can glean something from these words that is meaningful and helpful to their understanding of their parents.

The family on the farm where Ally grew up celebrating her father's 100th birthday. Vernon would be proud.

BIBLIOGRAPHY

BOOKS

Stephen E. Ambrose, *Crazy Horse and Custer*, New York, Open Road Integrated Media, 1975

Atlas of the New West, University of Colorado, Boulder, CO, *The Atlas of the New West,* 1997

Bushton News, newspaper issue commemorating fiftieth anniversary of the city of Bushton, 1937

Bushton, Kansas, *Centennial publication*, 1987

Truman Capote, *In Cold Blood*, New York, Random House, Inc., 1965

Tony Castro, *The Best There Ever Was,* London, U.K., Roman & Littlefield, 2019

Ivan Doig, Work Song, New York, Penguin Publishing roup, 2010

M. T. Edvardsson, *A Nearly Normal Family*, Celadon Books, 2019

Robert Ellwood, *The Fifties Spiritual Marketplace: American Religion in a Decade of Conflict,* Rutgers University Press, 1997

Linda Gordon, *Woman's Body, Woman's Right: A Social History of Birth Control in America* (updated and republished in 2004 as *The Moral Property of Women: A History of Birth Control Politics in America*), Chicago, Illinois, University of Illinois Press, 1974

David Halberstam, *The Fifties,* New York, Open Road Integrated Media, 1993

James D. Horan and Paul Sann, *Pictorial History of the Wild West*, New York, Bonanza Books, 1954

Horace Jones, *The Story of Early Rice County,* Lyons, Kansas, Lyons Daily News, 1929

Andrew C. Isenberg, *The Destruction of the Bison*, Cambridge, UK, Cambridge University Press, 2000

Robert P Jones, *The End of White Christian America*, New York, Simon and Schuster, 2019

William Kittredge, *Owning it All,* Saint Paul, Minn., Graywolf Press, 1987

Arthur Koestler, *Darkness at Noon*, New York, New American Library of World Literature, 1941

Kevin Kruse. *One Nation Under God,* New York, Basic Books, 2015

William Least Heat-Moon, *PrairyErth*, Boston, Massachusetts, Houghton Mifflin Company, 1991

Larry Meredith, *Cast a Giant Shadow*, Gunnison, CO, Raspberry Creek Books, 2017

Marguerite Pattan, *Post War Kitchen: Nostalgic Food and Facts from 1945 to 1954*, United Kingdom, Hamlyn Publishing, 1998.

Jonathan Raban, *Bad Land*: *An American Romance,* New York, Vintage Books, 1996

Richard Rhodes, *The Making of the Atomic Bomb,* New York, Simon and Schuster, 1986

Richard Rhodes, *Farm: A Year in the Life of an American Farmer*, New York, Simon & Schuster, 1989
Sara Sheridan, *The World of Sanditon,* New York, Grand Central Publishing, 2019

Tory Telfer, *Lady Killers: deadly women throughout history*, New York, Harper Collins, 2017

Andrea Tone, *Devices and Desires: A History of Contraceptives in America, New York,* Hill and Wang, 2001

Amor Towles, *A Gentleman in Moscow,* New York, Viking, 2016

Mark Twain, *The Adventures of Huckleberry Finn,* United Kingdom, 1884

John Updike, *Of the Farm,* Alfred A. Knopf, Inc., 1965

J. D. Vance, *Hillbilly Elegy: A memoir of a family and culture in crisis,* New York, Harper Collins, 2016

Walter Prescott Webb, *The Great Plains*, New York, University of Nebraska Press, 1931

Tara Westover, *Educated: A Memoir.* New York, Random House, 2018

Beatriz Williams, *The Golden Hour,* New York, Harper Collins, 2019

WEBSITES

https://www.allhighschools.com/school/bushton-high-school/999034081
https://www.allure.com/story/history-of-birth-control
https://www.answers.com/Q/What_is_the_cost_of_a_gallon_of_gasoline_in_1957
https://www.archives.datapages.com/data/bulletns/1931-37/data/pg/0019/0010/1400/1405.htm

https://blog.education.nationalgeographic.org/2018/09/16/what-is-westward-expansion/
https://www.britannica.com/topic/McCarthyism
https://datausa.io/profile/geo/bushton-ks/
https://www.eia.gov/state/analysis.php?sid=KS
https://en.wikipedia.org/wiki/Agricultural_Adjustment_Act
https://en.wikipedia.org/wiki/Great_Plains_Shelterbelt
https://en.wikipedia.org/wiki/History_of_the_St._Louis_Browns
https://en.wikipedia.org/wiki/Kansas_State_University
https://en.wikipedia.org/wiki/Marlon_Brando

https://en.wikipedia.org/wiki/United_States_in_the_1950s#Popular_culture_and_mass_media

https://en.wikipedia.org/wiki/Wheat_production_in_the_United_States

https://healthtopquestions.com/newly-released-cancer-data
https://www.history.com/topics/cold-war/1950s

https://images.search.yahoo.com/search/images;_ylt=Awr9H6oMcmVdV6IAnpFXNyoA;_ylu=X3oDMTEyanFiZjI2BGNvbG8DZ3ExBHBvcwMxBHZ0aWQDQjY4MzNfMQRzZWMDc2M-?p=Bushton%2C+KS&fr=yfp-t

https://www.imdb.com/name/nm0000008/bio?ref_=nm_dyk_qt_sm#quotes

https://infosys.ara.usda.gov/WindErosion/symposium/proceedings/able.pdf
http://www.ipsr.ku.edu/ksdata/ksah/energy/oilmap.pdf
https://www.kansasmemory.org/iem/210637
https://kansastreespade.com/windbreak-construction/

https://www.khanacademy.org/humanities/us-history/postwarera/1950s-america/a/popular-culture-and-mass-media-cnx

https://www.kshs.org/kansapedia/agriculture-in-kansas/14188
https://learningenglish.voanews.com/a/america-nineteen-fifties-family-life/1263187.html
https://www.legacy.com/obituaries/dodgeglobe/obituary.aspx?pid=174293806

https://www.legacy.com/obituaries/dodgeglobe/obituary.aspx?pid=174293806

https://livinghistoryfarm.org/farminginthe50s/machines_01.html

https://www.nass.usda.gov/Statistics_by_State/Kansas/Publications/Cooperative_Projects/KS_wheat2017.pdf

http://nationalfestivalofbreads.com/nutrition-education/wheat-facts

https://www.northernnaturalgas.com/INFOPOSTINGS/Pages/Locations.aspx

https://www.nps.gov/safe/planyourvisit/maps.htm

https://www.ndstudies.gov/gr4/north-dakota-agriculture/part-1-north-dakota-agriculture/section-17-modern-farming-arrives-1945

https://prezi.com/t0oplvpop3le/religion-in-the-1940s-and-1950s

https://www.reference.com/education/school-like-1950s-eb5e60b06351577e

https://www.retrowaste.com/1950s/sports-in-the-1950s/

https://theconversation.com

https://search.yahoo.com/search?p=geological+history+of+Kansas&fr=yfp-t&fp=1&toggle=1&cop=mss&ei=UTF-8

http://www.thepeoplehistory.com/1957.html

https://tvtropes.org/pmwiki/pmwiki.php/Main/TheFifties

http://weather.gov/ict/topten

OTHER
U.S. Census Bureau
President Theodore Roosevelt's Commission on Country Life, 1909
Grain and Feed Statistics Report, U.S. Department of Agriculture, 1965
Lyle Meredith obituary, *Dodge City Globe,* 2015
Newsweek Magazine, May, 1954

ABOUT "US"

A picture of Larry and Ally on a hike on Independence Pass at nearly 12,000 feet *(Photo by Lauren Meredith)*. The pass is just outside of Aspen and not far from Redstone near where they now live. Redstone is in the Crystal River Valley and near where their daughter Suzy and her husband Denny live, and only a few miles farther on to the home of their son Greg, his wife Tina and their children Jack and Lauren. Larry's family had often visited relatives in or near the valley and his parents purchased a home there in the mid-'60s. Living there became a dream for all – a dream that has now been realized.

To get to this point Larry has been a newspaperman, a salesman, an advertising and sales promotion writer for a Fortune 500 company, a university administrator and teacher, has owned his own marketing and video production company and has served as the Executive Director of a library district and the Director of the Publishing Certificate program at Western Colorado University. He also served in the U.S. Army. He earned an MA degree in English Literature in 1971. He has written hundreds of published essays and newspaper and magazine articles and is the author of the historical novel *This Cursed Valley* and the biography *Cast a Giant Shadow: Hollywood Movie Great Ted White and the Evolution of American Movies and TV in the 20th Century*.

Ally also has a Master's Degree (from Grand Canyon University in Arizona). She has been a K-12 music specialist and was the Collaborative Pianist for the Department of Music at Western Colorado University. She has been the pianist for a number of churches, formed and directed church handbell choirs and has been a member of, and soloist for, many musical ensembles including the Gunnison Opera Study Group. At Western Colorado University she guided many students as they prepared for careers as instrumental performers or opera singers. She continues to use her musical talents for area churches and as a member of such groups as the Aspen Choral Society.

Larry on his 80th birthday with grandchildren Jack, left, and Lauren.

www.ingramcontent.com/pod-product-compliance
Lightning Source LLC
Chambersburg PA
CBHW030442300426
44112CB00009B/1119